*Insight Phrase Book*
# French
*Original text:* Elisabeth Graf-Riemann
*Editor:* Sabine von Loeffelholz
*English edition translated by:* Paul Fletcher
*Edited by:* Renée Holler and Clare Peel

*Managing Editor:* Tony Halliday
*Editorial Director:* Brian Bell

**CONTACTING THE EDITORS:** As every effort is made to provide accurate information in this publication, we would appreciate it if readers would call our attention to any errors and omissions by contacting:
*Apa Publications, PO Box 7910, London SE1 1WE, England.*
*Fax: (44 20) 7403 0290*
*e-mail: insight@apaguide.demon.co.uk*

Information has been obtained from sources believed to be reliable,
but its accuracy and completeness, and the opinions based thereon,
are not guaranteed.

© 2000 APA Publications GmbH & Co. Verlag KG Singapore Branch, Singapore.

*1st edition 2000, Reprinted 2002*

*Printed in Singapore by Insight Print Services (Pte) Ltd*

*Original edition © Polyglott-Verlag Dr Bolte KG, Munich*

Distributed in the UK & Ireland by:
**GeoCenter International Ltd**
The Viables Centre, Harrow Way, Basingstoke,
Hampshire RG22 4BJ
Tel: (44 1256) 817987, Fax: (44 1256) 817-988

Distributed in the United States by:
**Langenscheidt Publishers, Inc.**
46–35 54th Road, Maspeth, NY 11378
Tel: (1 718) 784-0055, Fax: (1 718) 784-0640

Worldwide distribution enquiries:
**APA Publications GmbH & Co. Verlag KG (Singapore Branch)**
38 Joo Koon Road, Singapore 628990
Tel: (65) 865-1600, Fax: (65) 861-6438

# INSIGHT PHRASE BOOK

# FRENCH

**APA PUBLICATIONS**

Part of the Langenscheidt Publishing Group

# Contents

# Introduction

## About this book

Insight Phrase Books are the perfect companions when touring abroad as they cover all the everyday situations faced by travellers who are not familiar with the language of their holiday hosts.

The sentences and expressions translated here have been chosen carefully so that you can make yourself understood quickly and easily. You will not find any complicated sentence constructions or long word lists. Nearly all the sentences have been compiled from basic phrases so that by substituting words and other expressions, you will be able to cope with a variety of conversational situations.

The word lists at the end of each section are themed and this will make it easy for you to vary what you want to say. You will be able to make yourself understood quickly in the foreign language with the minimum vocabulary. You won't need to spend a long time searching for the word you want.

So that you can understand what others are saying to you in everyday situations, e.g. at the doctor, at the border, we have marked with a * those phrases and questions that you are likely to hear frequently.

A simplified pronunciation guide geared towards English speakers will help you to say correctly the words you need. You will also find a summary of basic pronunciation information, together with a brief introduction to French grammar.

This introduction is followed by nine chapters containing examples of sentences from general and tourist-related situations. You will find general tips and guidance not just in the chapter entitled Practical Information, but elsewhere in the book too. The various feature boxes contain useful information on such matters as meal times, using public transport and telephones, the different categories of hotels and restaurants and lots more.

At the end of the book you will find a English-French dictionary, which can be used for reference and as an index, the page number referring to an entry in one of the nine chapters. The French-English dictionary contains a selection of important words and abbreviations that you are likely to encounter on signs, notices and information boards.

Hoping you have lots of fun on your travels and Bon voyage! [bõ vwayazh] *(Have a good trip!)*

## Pronunciation

All the French words included in this guide are given a phonetic rendering. This always appears in square brackets after the translation.

Although the phonetic rendering can be read as though it were English, the following points about pronunciation should be noted:

### Vowels

The nasal vowel is a distinctive feature of the French language and there is no similar sound in English, although many people will be familiar with the pronunciation of such words as bonjour, Cointreau and vin. It occurs when vowels are followed by n or m. To describe this sound, uttered through the nose and the mouth at the same time, we have used the following symbols: ã, õ and ũ.

– ã (in French either -ain, -ein or -in) represents the a in bat combined with the nasal sound, e.g. vin [vã] *(wine).*

– õ (in French -an, -am or -en) represents the o in lot combined with the nasal sound, e.g. plan [plõ] *(plan)*. The French -on is pronounced similarly e.g. pardon [pardõ] *(sorry)*
– ũ (in French -un) describes the u in cut but combined with the nasal sound, e.g. un [ũ] *(a, one)*

To practise the pronunciation of the nasal vowel, try saying this sentence:

– õ Dans ta tente ta tante t'attend [dõ ta tõt ta tõt tatõ] *(Your aunt is waiting for you in your tent)*.

## Consonants

The other difficulty for English speakers is the -r sound. It is created by rolling the tongue at the back of the throat. In this book we do not differentiate between the English r and the French r.

Listed below are a number of points to help you with the pronunciation of other consonants:

– the c is pronounced as a k before a, o and u, unless it has a cedilla (ç), e.g. cacao [kakow] *(chocolate)*.
– ç and c before e and i are not voiced, e.g. France [frõs] *(France)*; français [frõsay] *(French)*
– g followed by e or i is a voiced sh sound as in the English word pleasure, e.g. gentil [zhõtee] *(kind)*
– g followed by a, o and u is hard, as in the English get, e.g. garçon [garsõ] *(boy)*
– gn is pronounced like the ni in the English word onion, e.g. Espagne [espanyuh] *(Spain)*
– h is always silent, e.g. hôtel [otel] *(hotel)*
– s between vowels is voiced, e.g. chose [shoz] *(thing)*
– qu is pronounced like a k, e.g. quand [kõ] *(when)*
– w is rarely used in French. When it occurs, it is usually pronounced as a v, e.g. wagon [vagõ] *(carriage)*
– y is normally pronounced as ee, e.g. hypermarché [eepermarshay] *(hypermarket)*

– x at the end of words is an s sound, six [sees] *(six)*, otherwise as in English, e.g. example [egzõpl] *(example)*

The final consonant is rarely spoken, e.g. le tapis [luh tapee] *(the carpet)*. However, if the following word begins with a vowel, then the final consonant is slurred into the following vowel and voiced, e.g. les enfants [layz‿õfõ] *(the children)*.

## Accents

Accents above the e change its pronunciation. An é (acute accent) represents a closed sound, e.g. café [kafay] *(coffee, café)*. An è (grave accent) is a more open sound, e.g. mère [mair] *(mother)*. This sound is similar to that created by ê (circumflex accent), e.g. même [mem] *(same)*. Accents occur on other vowels, but make very little difference to the pronunciation.

## Emphasis

As a general rule a slight emphasis on French words usually goes on the last syllable of a word, e.g. repas [ruhpa] *(meal)*. An -e ending without an accent is not stressed, e.g. tante [tõt] *(aunt)*.

### The French alphabet

| | | | |
|---|---|---|---|
| a | [a] | n | [en] |
| b | [bay] | o | [oh] |
| c | [say] | p | [pay] |
| d | [day] | q | [kew] |
| e | [uh] | r | [air] |
| f | [ef] | s | [es] |
| g | [zhay] | t | [tay] |
| h | [ash] | u | [oo] |
| i | [ee] | v | [vay] |
| j | [zhee] | w | [doobluh vay] |
| k | [ka] | x | [eex] |
| l | [el] | y | [ee grek] |
| m | [em] | z | [zed] |

# French Grammar In Brief

## The article

All French nouns are either masculine *(m)* or feminine *(f)*. Even inanimate objects are one or the other. In some cases the noun ending will indicate whether a word is masculine or feminine, but more often than not there is no way of knowing.

### Definite article

| masculine singular | masculine plural |
|---|---|
| le jour [luh zhoor] | les jours [lay zhoor] |
| *(the day)* | *(the days)* |
| feminine singular | feminine plural |
| la rue [la roo] | les rues [lay roo] |
| *(the street)* | *(the streets)* |

### Indefinite article

| masculine singular | masculine plural |
|---|---|
| un jour [ū zhoor] | des jours [day zhoor] |
| *(a day)* | *(some days)* |
| feminine singular | feminine plural |
| une rue [oon roo] | des rues [day roo] |
| *(a street)* | *(some streets)* |

When nouns begin with a vowel or a silent h, then the masculine and feminine definite article is reduced to l' :

l'avion *(m)* [lavyõ] *(the aeroplane)*; l'heure *(f)* [luhr] *(the time/hour)*.

The final letter of the singular indefinite masculine article (un) and the plural articles (les and des) flows into nouns:

un avion [ūn‿avyõ] *(an aeroplane)*; les avions [lays‿avyõ] *(the aeroplanes)*; des heures [dayz‿uhr] *(hours)*.

## Quantities with de

Nouns and expressions of quantity are always followed by de [duh]: une tasse de café [oon tas duh kafay] *(a cup of coffee)*; beaucoup de pommes [bohkoo duh pom] *(a lot of apples)*.

## Nouns

Sometimes a noun ending can help with determining gender.

Nouns that end with -**ment** [mõ] and -**eur** [uhr] are generally masculine: le renseignement [rõsaynyuhmõ] *(information)*; le coiffeur [kwafuhr] *(hairdresser)*.

Nouns ending in -**ion** [-yõ] and -**euse** [-uhz] are always feminine, e.g. la location [la lokasyõ] *(rental)*; la dépanneuse [la depanuhz] *(breakdown truck)*.

### Forming plurals

Most nouns form their plural, as in English, by adding -**s**, but it is not normally pronounced, e.g. le jour [luh zhoor] *(the day)* – les jours [lay zhoor] *(the days)*; la limonade [leemonad] *(the lemonade)* – les limonades [lay leemonad] *(the lemonades)*. Nouns that end with -**au**, -**eau** or -**ou**, form their plurals by adding an -**x**, but this is not pronounced either: le château [luh shato] *(the castle)* – les châteaux [lay shato] *(the castles)*. Nouns that already end in -**s**, -**z** or -**x**, remain unchanged, e.g. le tapis [luh tapee] *(the carpet)* – les tapis [lay tapee] *(the carpets)*; le nez [luh nay] *(the nose)* – les nez [lay nay] *(the noses)*; le prix [luh pree] *(the price)* – les prix [lay pree] *(the prices)*.

## Adjectives

The adjective always agrees with the noun, even if it does not adjoin the noun: un bon repas [ū bõ ruhpa] *(a good meal)*; le repas est bon [luh ruhpa e bõ] *(the meal is good)*.

The feminine form of the adjective is usually formed by adding an -**e** to the masculine form, e.g. le grand garçon [luh grõ garsõ] *(the tall boy)*, but: la grande maison [la grõd mayzõ] *(the large house)*. When an -**e** follows a consonant, then that consonant is sounded: vert [vair] – verte [vairt] *(green)*.

If the masculine form ends in an -**n** or -**s**, then this consonant is doubled before the -**e**: bon [bõ] – bonne [bon] *(good)*; gros [gro] – grosse [gros] *(big)*.

## Forming plurals

To form the plural of the adjective, an -**s** is added to the masculine and feminine singular form. Again, this -**s** is not pronounced: le grand garçon [luh grõ garsõ] *(the tall boy)* – les grands garçons [lay grõ garsõ] *(the tall boys)*; la grande maison [la grõd mayzõ] *(the large house)* – les grandes maisons [lay grõd maysõ] *(the large houses)*.

Important exceptions:
*beautiful:*
singular: beau *(m)* [boh] – belle *(f)* [bel]
plural: beaux *(m)* [boh] – belles *(f)* [bel]
*old:* singular: vieux *(m)* [vyuh] – vieille *(f)* [vyay]
plural: vieux *(m)* [vyuh] – vieilles *(f)* [vyay]

In the following chapters the masculine form of the adjective will be shown first, with the feminine ending after the comma, e.g. Je suis désolé, -e [zhuh swee dezolay] *(I'm sorry)*.

## Position of the adjective

The basic rule states that short (single-syllable) adjectives precede the noun, longer (multi-syllable) adjectives follow the noun, e.g. un bon café [ũ bõ kafay] *(a good coffee)*; un livre intéressant [ũ leevr ãteresõ] *(an interesting book)*. Adjectives of colour always follow the noun, e.g. le ciel bleu [luh syel bluh] *(the blue sky)*.

## Comparison of adjectives

Adjectives are compared by preceding the adjective with plus [ploo] *(more)*, e.g.

grand [grõ] *(large)* – plus grand [ploo grõ] *(larger)*.

The definite article is used to form the superlative, e.g. le plus grand [luh ploo grõ] *(the largest)*.

To make a direct comparison use que [kuh] *(than)*: Marcel est plus grand que Pascal. [marsel‿e ploo grõ kuh paskal] *(Marcel is taller than Pascal)*.

**Irregular comparisons:**
bon [bõ] *(good)* – meilleur [meyuhr] *(better)*;
mauvais [mohvay] *(bad)* – pire [peer] *(worse)*.

# Adverbs

Adverbs are usually formed by adding -**ment** to the feminine form of the adjective, e.g. forte [fort] – fortement [fortuhmõ] *(strongly)*

Bien [byã] *(well)* and mal [mal] *(badly)* are irregular adverbs.

# Pronouns

In English there is only one way of addressing people – with the word you. In French there are two ways. One is the polite, formal way (**vous**), the other more informal (**tu**).

**Tu** is used between friends, relatives, people of the same age group and to children. **Vous** is both the formal way to address someone, i.e. in most tourist transactions, and it is also the plural of **tu**.

The pronoun forms of tu are te [tuh] *(to you, you)*, ton [tõ] *(your; m)*, ta [ta] *(your; f)*, tes [tay] *(your; pl)*.

## Subject pronouns

(I, you, he, she etc)

je [zhuh] *(I)*
tu [too] *(you)*
il [eel] *(he)*, elle [el] *(she)*
nous [noo] *(we)*
vous [voo] *(you)*
ils [eel] *(they; m)*, elles [el] *(she; f)*

When followed by a word that begins with a vowel or a silent h, the subject pronoun **je** is shortened to **j'**, e.g. j'achète [zhashet] *(I buy)*; j'habite [zhabeet] *(I live)*.

### Object pronouns

(me, you, him etc)

me [muh] *(me)*
te [tuh] *(you)*
lui [loo-ee] *(to him, to her)*
le [luh] *(him, it)*
la [la] *(her, it)*
nous [noo] *(us)*
vous [voo] *(you)*
leur [luhr] *(to them)*
les [lay] *(them)*

When followed by a word which begins with a vowel or a silent h, the object pronouns me, te, le and la are shortened to m', t' and l': Je l'achète [zhuh lashet] *(I buy it)*.

### Possessive pronouns

(my, your, his etc)

Singular possessive pronouns agree with the gender of the noun which follows, not the gender of the owner, e.g. C'est son sac. [say sõ sak] *(It is his/her bag)*. C'est sa chambre [say sa shõbr] *(It is his/her room)*.

*masculine: feminine: plural:*
mon [mõ]   ma [ma]   mes [may]   *(my)*
ton [tõ]   ta [ta]   tes [tay]   *(yours)*
son [sõ]   sa [sa]   ses [say]   *(his; her)*
notre [notr]   nos [no]   *(our)*
votre [votr]   vos [vo]   *(your)*
leur [luhr]   leurs [luhr]   *(their)*

### Demonstrative pronoun

(this, that, these, those)

The masculine singular demonstrative pronoun is ce [suh], the feminine cette [set]: ce monsieur [suh muhsyuhr] *(this man)*; cette dame [set dam] *(this woman)*. When ce is followed by a masculine noun that begins with a vowel or a silent h, it becomes cet, e.g. cet enfant [set͜õnfõ] *(this child)*.

# The verb

The main auxiliary verbs are **to be** and **to have**:

être [etr] *(to be)*:
je suis [zhuh swee] *(I am)*
tu es [too ay] *(you are)*
il/elle est [eel/el ay] *(he/she is)*
nous sommes [noo som] *(we are)*
vous êtes [vooz͜et] *(you are)*
ils/elles sont [eel/el son] *(they are)*

avoir [avwar] *(to have)*:
j'ai [zhay] *(I have)*
tu as [too a] *(you have)*
il/elle a [eel/el a] *(he/she has)*
nous avons [nooz͜avõ] *(we have)*
vous avez [vooz͜avay] *(you have)*
ils/elles ont [eels͜õ/els͜õ] *(they have)*

There are three types of regular verbs in French. They are classified according to the ending of the infinitive form.

Regular verbs ending in -**er**:

donner [donay] *(to give)*:
je donne [zhuh don] *(I give)*
tu donnes [too don] *(you give)*
il/elle donne [eel/el don] *(he/she gives)*
nous donnons [noo donõ] *(we give)*
vous donnez [voo donay] *(you give)*
ils/elles donnent [eel/el don] *(they give)*

Many other commonly used verbs form part of this group. They include aimer [aymay] *(to like, to love)*; arriver [areevay] *(to arrive)*; habiter [abeetay] *(to live)*; jouer [zhoo-ay] *(to play)*; regarder [regarday] *(to look at)*; travailler [traviyay] *(to work)*; visiter [veeseetay] *(to visit)*.

Regular verbs ending in -**ir**:

finir [feeneer] *(to finish)*:
je finis [zhuh feenee] *(I finish)*
tu finis [too feenee] *(you finish)*
il/elle finit [eel/el feenee] *(he/she finishes)*
nous finissons [noo feeneesõ] *(we finish)*
vous finissez [voo feeneesay] *(you finish)*
ils/elles finissent [eel/el feenees] *(they finish)*

The verb choisir [shwazeer] *(to choose)* follows exactly the same pattern. Partir [parteer] *(to leave)* is similar:

je pars [zhuh par] *(I leave)*
tu pars [too par] *(you leave)*
il/elle part [eel/el par] *(he/she leaves)*
nous partons [noo partõ] *(we leave)*
vous partez [voo partay] *(you leave)*
ils/elles partent [eel/el part] *(they leave)*

Other verbs with endings like partir are dormir [dormeer] *(to sleep)*, servir [serveer] *(to serve)*.

The third group of regular verbs end with -**re**:

vendre [võdr] *(to sell)*:
je vends [zhuh võ] *(I sell)*
tu vends [too võ] *(you sell)*
il/elle vend [eel/el võ] *(he/she sells)*
nous vendons [noo võndõ] *(we sell)*
vous vendez [voo võday] *(you sell)*
ils/elles vendent [eel/el võd] *(they sell)*

Other common verbs in this grouping are répondre [repõdr] *(to answer)*; attendre [atõdr] *(to wait)*.

Several very commonly used verbs follow an irregular pattern.

aller [alay] *(to go)*:
je vais [zhuh vay] *(I go)*
tu vas [too va] *(you go)*
il/elle va [eel/el va] *(he/she goes)*
nous allons [nooz‿alõ] *(we go)*
vous allez [vooz‿alay] *(you go)*
ils/elles vont [eel/el võ] *(they go)*

devoir [devwa] *(to have to)*:
je dois [zhuh dwa] *(I must)*

tu dois [too dwa] *(you must)*
il/elle doit [eel/el dwa] *(he/she must)*
nous devons [noo devõ] *(we must)*
vous devez [voo devay] *(you must)*
ils/elles doivent [eel/el dwav] *(they must)*

faire [fair] *(to do, to make)*:
je fais [zhuh fay] *(I do)*
tu fais [too fay] *(you do)*
il/elle fait [eel/el fay] *(he/she does)*
nous faisons [noo fesõ] *(we do)*
vous faites [voo fet] *(you do)*
ils/elles font [eel/el fõ] *(they do)*

prendre [prõdr] *(to take)*:
je prends [zhuh prõ] *(I take)*
tu prends [too prõ] *(you take)*
il/elle prend [eel/el prõ] *(he/she takes)*
nous prenons [noo prenõ] *(we take)*
vous prenez [voo prenay] *(you take)*
ils/elles prennent [eel/el pren] *(they take)*

venir [veneer] *(to come)*:
je viens [zhuh vyã] *(I come)*
tu viens [too vyã] *(you come)*
il/elle vient [eel/el vyã] *(he/she comes)*
nous venons [noo venõ] *(we come)*
vous venez [voo venay] *(we come)*
ils/elles viennent [eel/el vyen] *(they come)*

## Negatives

To form a negative, the verb is enclosed by either **ne ... pas** [nuh ... pa] *(not)*, **ne ... jamais** [nuh ... zhamay] *(never)*, **ne ... rien** [nuh ... ryõ] *(nothing)*, **ne ... plus** [nuh ... ploo] *(no longer)*, **ne ... personne** [nuh ... pairson] *(nobody)*: Je ne travaille pas [zhuh nuh traviy pa] *(I don't work)*. Il ne boit jamais [eel nuh bwa zhamay] *(He never drinks.)*

Note that **ne** is shortened to **n'** when the following verb begins with a vowel or a silent h, e.g. Nous n'attendons plus. [noo natõndõ ploo] *(We are not waiting any longer.)*

## Asking questions

There are three ways to ask questions:
1. By raising the voice at the end of the sentence: Vous louez des bicyclettes? [voo loo-ay day beeseeklet] *(Do you hire out bikes?)*
2. By preceding the verb with **Est-ce que**, e.g. Est-ce que vous êtes seul? [eskuh vooz‿et suhl] *(Are you on your own?)*
3. By reversing subject and verb: Avez-vous une chambre? [avay vooz‿oon shõbr] *(Have you a room?)*

11

*Bonjour Madame!*
*Bonjour Monsieur!*
*Welcome*
*to France!*

# General

## Hello and goodbye

| | |
|---|---|
| Good morning/afternoon. | Bonjour. [bōzhoor] |
| Good evening. | Bonsoir. [bōswa] |
| Good night. | Bonne nuit. [bon‿nwee] |
| Hello! | Salut! [saloo] |
| How are you doing? | Comment ça va? [komō sa va] |
| How are you? | Comment allez-vous?/Comment vas-tu? [komōt‿alay voo/komō va too] |
| * Bien, merci. [byã mairsee] | Fine, thank you. |
| And you? | Et vous/toi? [ay voo/twa] |
| Goodbye. | Au revoir. [oh ruhvwa] |
| Bye/See you. | Salut. [saloo] |
| See you soon. | A bientôt. [a byãto] |
| See you tomorrow. | A demain. [a duhmã] |
| Regards to the family. | Amitiés à la famille. [ameetyay a la famee] |
| Thank you for everything. | Merci beaucoup pour tout. [mairsee bohkoo poor too] |
| We really enjoyed it. | Nous avons beaucoup aimé. [nooz‿avõ bohkoo aymay] |
| * Bon voyage! [bõ vwayazh] | Have a good journey! |

## Introducing yourself

| | |
|---|---|
| Mr/Mrs/Miss ... | Monsieur/Madame/Mademoiselle ... [muhsyuh/madam/madmwazel] |
| What's your name? | Vous vous appelez comment?/Tu t'appelles comment? [voo vooz‿apuhlay komõ/too tapel komõ] |
| My name is ... | Je m'appelle ... [zhuh mapel] |

**This is/These are**
my husband/my boyfriend
my wife/my girlfriend
my children.

**Voilà** [vwala]
mon mari/mon ami [mõ maree/mon‿amee]
ma femme/mon amie [ma fam/mon‿amee]
mes enfants. [mes‿õfõ]

Pleased to meet you.
And you.
Where are you from?

Enchanté. [õshõtay]
De même. [duh mem]
D'où es-tu/êtes-vous? [doo ay too/et voo]

**I'm/We're**
from England
from the USA
from Australia

**Je suis/Nous sommes** [zhuh swee/noo som]
d'Angleterre [dõngluhtair]
des États-Unis [dayz‿aytaz‿oonee]
d'Australie [dohstralee]

## Communication

Do you speak English?
What's that called in French?

Parlez-vous anglais? [parlay voo/parl too õnglay]
Comment est-ce que ça se traduit en français?
[komõ eskuh sa‿suh tradwee õ frõsay]

Pardon?/Sorry?
What does that mean?
Did you understand that?

Comment? [komõ]
Qu'est-ce que ça veut dire? [keskuh sa vuh deer]
Avez-vous/As-tu compris?
[avay voo/a too kõpree]

I don't understand.
Could you speak more slowly, please?

Je ne comprends pas. [zhuh nuh kõprõ pa]
Plus lentement, s'il vous plaît!
[ploo lõtmõ seel voo play]

Could you repeat that, please?

Répétez, s'il vous plaît! [repetay seel voo play]

### Bonjour, ça va?

A peck to the right, a peck to the left, right, left ... between friends, this ritual is often carried out between two and four times. Whether it's at home or in the streets, the fleeting kiss on the cheeks indicates not just family ties but also a close friendly relationship.

In a more formal situation, then the usual greeting is **bonjour Madame** [bõzhoor madam], **bonjour Monsieur** [bõzhoor muhsyuh]. If it is just the assistant in the bakery shop, then a cheery **ça va?** [sa va] (How are you?) will suffice to keep on good terms. The normal reply is **ça va** [sa va] (I'm fine) or perhaps even **ça va bien** [sa va byã] (I'm very well). If something is the matter, then the opposite response is **ça va mal** [sa va mal] (not so good).

The translation for please depends on how well you know the person you are speaking to. In English there is only one

way of addressing people using the word "you". In French there are two ways. **Vous** [voo] is more polite and used in formal situations and when speaking to more than one person; **tu** [too] is for use in informal situations when speaking to one person. A mother speaking to her son would use **tu**, but when speaking to all the family, she would use **vous**.

**S'il te plaît** [seel tuh play] is the informal way to say please and is used between friends and relatives and people of the same age group and also to children, while **s'il vous plaît** is the formal way. Most of the phrases in this book use the formal way of saying "you".

**Merci** [mairsee] is the word for thank you. Many waiters and shop assistants, for example, will then respond with **pas de quoi** [pa duh kwa] or **de rien** [duh ryã], both of which correspond with "you're welcome" or "not at all".

13

| Could you … for me? | Pourriez-vous/Pourrais-tu me |
|---|---|
| | [pooree-ay voo/pooray too muh] |
| write that down | l'écrire [laykreer] |
| explain/translate that | l'expliquer/le traduire? [lexpleekay/luh tradweer] |

## Civilities

| Please. | S'il vous plaît. [seel voo play] |
|---|---|
| Thank you/Thank you very much. | Merci./Merci beaucoup. [mairsee/mairsee bohkoo] |
| Thank you, the same to you. | Merci, de même. [mairsee duh mem] |
| Thank you very much for all your help. | Je vous remercie de votre aide. [zhuh voo ruhmairsee duh votr_ed] |
| * Pas de quoi. [pa duh kwa] | You're welcome. |
| Sorry/Excuse me. | Pardon./Excusez moi. [pardõ/exkoosay mwa] |
| * Ça ne fait rien. [sa_nuh fay ryã] | It doesn't matter./Don't worry. |
| Wait a moment, please! | Un instant, s'il vous plaît! [ũn_ãstõ seel voo play] |
| That's very nice of you. | C'est très gentil à vous. [say tray zhõtee a voo] |
| I'm sorry about that. | Je suis désolé,-e. [zhuh swee dezolay] |
| That's a pity. | C'est dommage. [say domazh] |
| Welcome! | Bienvenue! [byãvuhnoo] |
| Congratulations! | Félicitations! [fayleeseetasyõ] |
| Happy birthday! | Bon anniversaire! [bon_aneevairsair] |
| Get well soon! | Un bon rétablissement! [ũ bõ raytableesmõ] |
| Good luck! | Bonne chance! [bon shõs] |
| Have a nice day! | Bonne journée! [bon zhoornay] |
| Have a good journey! | Bon voyage! [bõ vwayazh] |
| Have a good holiday! | Bonnes vacances! [bon vakõs] |
| Merry Christmas! | Joyeux Noël! [zhwayuh noel] |
| Happy Easter! | Joyeux Pâques! [zhwayuh pak] |
| Happy New Year! | Bonne année! [bon_anay] |

## Meeting people

| Do you mind if I sit here? | Puis-je m'asseoir ici? [pweezhuh maswa eesee] |
|---|---|
| Do you mind? | Vous permettez? [voo pairmetay] |

| Are you | Vous êtes/Tu es [vooz_et/too e] |
|---|---|
| on you own | seul,-e [suhl] |
| with somebody | accompagné,-e [akõpanyay] |
| married? | marié,-e? [maryay] |

| Do you have a boyfriend/girlfriend? | As-tu un ami/une amie? [a too ũn_amee/oon_amee] |
|---|---|
| How old are you? | Quel âge as-tu? [kel azh a too] |
| I am 25 years old. | J'ai vingt-cinq ans. [zhay vã sãk_ã] |
| What do you do for a living? | Quelle est votre/ta profession? [kel ay votr/ta profesyõ] |

14

## argot = slang

As in every living language there are countless French expressions in everyday use which do not appear in any dictionary. Sometimes it is difficult to be sure where the dividing line is between acceptable usage and colloquial language, or **argot** [argo], as the French call it. So **la voiture** [la vwatoor] for the car often becomes **la bagnole** [la banyol], **le travail** [luh travay] or work is invariably **le boulôt** [luh boolo], and **l'argent** [larzhõ], the French for money, is **le fric** [luh freek].

Many common words are shortened. **Sympathique** [săpateek] meaning nice is often reduced to **sympa** [săpa]. Le **professeur** [luh profesuhr] can mean both the school-teacher or the university professor but he is often simply **le prof** [luh prof]. **Le restaurant** [luh restorõ] regularly becomes **le resto** [luh restoh] and **le frigidaire** [luh freezheedair], which is French for refrigerator, is almost always **le frigo** [luh freego].

If you go into a clothes shop, you will probably see **le pull** [luh pul] for **le pullover** [luh pullovair] and at the restaurant you may well be asked if you want to start the meal with **un apéro** [ũn‿apero] instead of **l'apéritif** [ũn‿apereeteef].

| | |
|---|---|
| I'm still at school. | Je vais encore au lycée. [zhuh vayz‿ōkor‿oh leesay] |
| I'm a student. | Je suis étudiant (étudiante). [juh sweez‿aytoodyõ (aytoodyõt)] |
| I'm employed. | Je suis employé. [zhuh sweez‿õplwayay] |
| Can I buy you a drink? | Vous désirez boire quelque chose? [voo dayzeeray bwa kelk shoz] |
| Thank you, that would be nice. | Oui, volontiers, bonne idée. [wee volõtyay bon‿eeday] |
| No, thank you. | Non, merci. [nõ mairsee] |
| Perhaps another time. | Peut-être une autre fois. [puhtaitre‿ũn‿ohtr fwa] |
| Maybe later. | Peut-être plus tard. [puhtaitre ploo tar] |
| Do you like it here? | Vous vous plaisez/Tu te plais ici? [voo voo plesay/too tuh playz‿eesee] |
| I like it very much here. | Je me plais beaucoup ici. [zhuh muh play bohkoo eesee] |
| Is this your first time here? | C'est la première fois que vous venez/tu viens ici? [say la premyair fwa kuh voo venay/too vyã eesee] |
| No, I've been to ... before. | Non, j'étais déjà à ... [nõ zhetay dayzha a] |
| Have you ever been to England? | Connaissez-vous/Connais-tu l'Angleterre? [konesay voo/konay too lõgluhtair] |
| Come and visit me. | Venez me/Viens me voir un de ces jours. [venay muh/vyã muh vwa ũ duh say zhoor] |
| Here's my address. | Voici mon adresse. [vwasee mon‿adres] |
| How long have you been staying here? | Combien de temps est-ce que vous êtes/tu es déjà ici? [kõbyã duh tõ eskuh vooz‿et/too ay dayzha eesee] |
| For a week./For two days. | Depuis une semaine/deux jours. [duhpwee oon suhmen/duh zhoor] |
| How much longer are you staying? | Vous resterez/Tu resteras encore combien de temps? [voo restuhray/too restuhra õkor kõbyã duh tõ] |

Another week/two days.

Encore une semaine/deux jours.
[ōkor⌣oon suhmen/duh zhoor]

**Shall we ... together today/tomorrow?**

**Nous pourrions ... ensemble, aujourd'hui/ demain?** [noo pooryō ōsōbl ... ozhoordwee/duhmā]

  have lunch

  déjeuner [dayzhuhnay]

  have dinner

  dîner [deenay]

  go out

  sortir [sorteer]

  go to the cinema/go dancing

  aller au cinéma/aller danser
  [alay oh seenayma/alay dōsay]

  do something sporty

  faire du sport [fair doo spor]

  play ...

  jouer [zhoo-ay]

O.K. (I'd like to)!

D'accord, je veux bien! [dakor zhuh vuh byā]

No, I don't want to.

Non, je ne veux pas. [nō zhuh nuh vuh pa]

I can't, sorry.

Je suis désolé. Je ne peux pas.
[zhuh swee dayzolay. zhuh nuh puh pa]

What time/Where shall we meet?

A quelle heure/Où est-ce que nous nous retrouverons?
[a kel⌣uhr/oo eskuh noo noo ruhtroovuhrō]

**Shall I**

**Je peux** [zhuh puh]

  pick you up

  passer vous/te prendre [passay voo/tuh prōdr]

  take you home

  vous/t'accompagner à la maison
  [voo/t⌣akōpanyay a la maysō]

  take you to the bus stop?

  vous/t'accompagner à l'arrêt d'autobus?
  [voo/t⌣akōpanyay a laray dohtoboos]

No, that's not necessary.

Non, ce n'est pas la peine.
[nō suh neh pa la pen]

It's been very nice.

J'ai beaucoup aimé. [zhay bohkoo aymay]

When can we see each other again?

Quand est-ce que nous nous reverrons?
[kōd⌣eskuh noo noo ruhverō]

I don't like that.

Je n'aime pas ça. [zhuh naym pa sa]/
Ça ne me plaît pas. [sa nuh muh play pa]

I don't feel like it.

Je n'en ai pas envie. [zhuh nōn⌣ay pas⌣ōvee]

Leave me alone!

Laissez-moi/Laisse-moi tranquille!
[laysay mwa/lays mwa trōkeel]

Please go away!

S'il vous plaît, partez/pars!
[seel voo play partay/par]

Get lost!

Disparaissez!/Disparais! [deesparesay/deesparay]

## Questions

What's that?

Qu'est-ce que c'est? [keskuh say]

How much is that?

Ça fait combien? [sa fay kōbyā]

Where is ... there?

Où est-ce qu'il y a ...? [oo esk⌣eelya]

Where does ... go?

Où va ...? [oo va]

What does that mean?

Qu'est-ce que ça veut dire? [keskuh sa vuh deer]

How long does it last?

Cela prend combien de temps?
[suhla prō kōbyā duh tō]

When does the concert start?

Le concert commence à quelle heure?
[luh kōsair komōs⌣a kel⌣uhr]

| | |
|---|---|
| How many kilometres is it? | C'est combien de kilomètres?<br>[say kōbyā duh keelometr] |

**Can you**
  help me
  show me, please?

**Pouvez-vous** [poovay voo]
  m'aider [mayday]
  me le montrer? [muh luh mōtray]

Can I help you?

Puis-je vous aider? [pweezhuh vooz–ayday]

## Interrogatives

| | |
|---|---|
| What? | Quoi? [kwa] |
| Who? | Qui? [kee] |
| Which? | Quel,-le? [kel] |
| Where? | Où? [oo] |
| How? | Comment? [komō] |
| How much/how many? | Combien (de)? [kōbyā (duh)] |
| When? | Quand? [kō] |
| How long? | Combien de temps? [kōbyā duh tō] |
| Why?/What ... for? | Pourquoi?/A quoi? [poorkwa/a kwa] |

## Time

| | |
|---|---|
| What's the time, please? | Quelle heure est-il, s'il vous plaît?<br>[kel–uhr–eteel seel voo play] |

**It's**
  one o'clock/two o'clock
  quarter past three
  quarter to five

  twenty past three
  half past three
  five to six
  noon/midnight.

**Il est** [eel–ay]
  une heure/deux heures [oon–uhr/duhz–uhr]
  trois heures et quart [trwaz–uhr–ay kar]
  cinq heures moins le quart
  [sāk–uhr mwā luh kar]
  quinze heures vingt [kāz–uhr vā]
  trois heures et demie [trwaz–uhr–ay duhmee]
  six heures moins cinq [sees–uhr mwā sāk]
  midi/minuit. [meedee/meenwee]

17

| | |
|---|---|
| What time do we have to be there? | A quelle heure faut-il arriver? [a kel‿uhr foht‿eel‿areevay] |
| Around twelve./At twelve o'clock sharp. | Vers midi./A midi juste. [vair meedee. a meedee zhoost] |
| When is breakfast/lunch/dinner? | A quelle heure y a-t-il le petit déjeuner/le déjeuner/le dîner? [a kel‿uhr yateel luh puhtee dayzhuhnay/luh dayzhuhnay/luh deenay] |
| * De huit à neuf heures. [duh weet‿a nuhf‿uhr] | From eight to nine. |

## Date

| | |
|---|---|
| What's the date today? | On est le combien aujourd'hui? [õn‿ay luh kõbyã ozhoordwee] |
| Today's the 1st/2nd/15th of August. | Aujourd'hui, on est le premier/deux/quinze août. [ozhoordwee õn‿ay luh pruhmee-ay/duh/kãz‿oot] |
| We'll arrive on the 20th of May. | Nous arriverons le vingt mai. [noos‿areeverõ luh vã meh] |
| We're staying until August 31st. | Nous resterons jusqu'au trente et un août. [noo restrõ zhooskoh trõt‿ay‿ũn‿oot] |
| I was born on January 12th (1960) | Je suis né,-e le douze janvier (mille neuf cent soixante). [zhuh swee nay luh dooz zhõvee-ay (meel nuhf sõ swasõt)] |
| My birthday is on January 12th. | Mon anniversaire est le douze janvier. [mon‿aneeversair ay luh dooz zhõvee-ay] |

## Indication of time

| | |
|---|---|
| in the morning | le matin [luh matã] |
| in the afternoon | l'après-midi (f) [lapray meedee] |
| in the evening | le soir [luh swa] |
| at the weekend | le week-end [luh weekend] |
| until tomorrow | à demain [a duhmã] |
| yesterday | hier [ee-air] |
| today | aujourd'hui [ozhoordwee] |
| tomorrow | demain [duhmã] |
| tonight | ce soir [suh swa] |
| day after tomorrow | après-demain [apray duhmã] |
| (two days) ago | il y a (deux jours) [eelya (duh zhoor)] |
| day before yesterday | avant-hier [avõt‿ee-air] |
| in a fortnight | dans quinze jours [dõ kãz zhoor] |
| this year/next year/last year/every year | cette année/l'année prochaine/l'année dernière/tous les ans [set‿anay/lanay proshen/lanay dernyair/too layz‿õ] |
| now | maintenant [mãtnõ] |
| sometimes | parfois [parfwa] |
| at midday | à midi [a meedee] |
| at night | la nuit [la nwee] |
| in time | à l'heure [a luhr] |
| since today/a week ago | depuis aujourd'hui/une semaine [duhpwee ohzhoordwee/oon suhmen] |

18

## Days of the week

Monday  lundi [lũdee]
Tuesday  mardi [mardee]
Wednesday  mercredi [mairkruhdee]
Thursday  jeudi [zhuhdee]
Friday  vendredi [võdruhdee]
Saturday  samedi [samdee]
Sunday  dimanche [deemõsh]

## Months

January  janvier [zhõvee-ay]
February  février [fevree-ay]
March  mars [mars]
April  avril [avreel]
May  mai [meh]

June  juin [zhwa]
July  juillet [zhwee-ay]
August  août [oot]
September  septembre [septõbr]
October  octobre [oktobr]
November  novembre [novõbr]
December  décembre [daysõbr]

## Seasons

spring  le printemps [luh prãtõ]
summer  l'été *(m)* [letay]
autumn  l'automne *(m)* [lohton]
winter  l'hiver *(m)* [leevair]
**peak season/off peak season**  la haute/basse saison [la oht/bas sayzõ]

| | |
|---|---|
| late/too late | tard/trop tard [tar/tro tar] |
| later | plus tard [ploo tar] |
| second | la seconde [la suhkõd] |
| minute | la minute [la meenoot] |
| hour | l'heure *(f)* [luhr] |
| daily | tous les jours [too lay zhoor] |
| day | le jour [luh zhoor] |
| week | la semaine [la suhmen] |
| before | avant [avõ] |
| during the morning | pendant la matinée [põdõ la mateenay] |
| at the moment | actuellement [akchoo-elmõ] |

## Weather

What a beautiful day!
Quelle belle journée!
[kel bel zhoornay]

Is it going to stay nice/bad?
Le mauvais/beau temps va continuer?
[luh mohvay/boh tõ va kõteenoo-ay]

What does the weather report say?
Quelles sont les prévisions météo?
[kel sõ lay prayveesyõ metayoh]

It's going to get colder/warmer.
Le temps se rafraîchit/se radoucit.
[luh tõ suh rafreshee/suh radoosee]

It is hot/close.
Il fait chaud/lourd. [il fä sho/lur]
It is windy/stormy/foggy.
Il y a du vent/une tempête/du brouillard.
[eelya doo võ/oon tõpet/doo broo-eeyar]

It is going to rain/snow today/tomorrow.
Aujourd'hui/Demain il va pleuvoir/neiger.
[ozhoordwee/duhmã eel va pluhvwa/nezhay]
For how long has it been raining?
Il pleut depuis quand? [il pluh duhpwee kõ]
When is it going to stop raining?
Quand est-ce que la pluie va s'arrêter?
[kõt̬eskuh la plwee va saretay]

| What's the temperature? | On a combien de degrés? |
| | [ōn‿a kōbyā duh duhgray] |
| 20° (in the shade). | Vingt degrés (à l'ombre). [vā duhgray (a lōbr)] |

## Measurements

| centimetre/metre/kilometre | le centimètre/le mètre/le kilomètre |
| | [luh sōteemetr/luh metr/luh keelometr] |
| square metre/square kilometre/hectare | le mètre carré/le kilomètre carré/l'hectare |
| | [luh metr karay/luh keelometr karay/l‿ektar] |
| cubic metre | le mètre cube [luh metr koob] |
| kilometres per hour | le kilomètre à l'heure [luh keelometr‿a luhr] |
| (quarter of a/half a/one) litre | (un quart de/un demi-/un) litre |
| | [(ū kar duh/ū demee/ū) leetr] |
| gram/pound/kilogramme/ton | le gramme/la livre/le kilo/la tonne |
| | [luh gram/la leevr/luh keelo/la ton] |
| second/minute/hour | la seconde/la minute/l'heure *(f)* |
| | [la suhkōd/la meenoot/luhr] |
| day/week/month/year | le jour/la semaine/le mois/l'an *(m)* |
| | [luh zhoor/la suhmen/luh mwa/lō] |
| a dozen/a couple/a portion | la douzaine/la paire/la portion |
| | [la doozen/la pair/la porsyō] |

## Colours

| I'm looking for a pair of blue/black trousers. | Je cherche un pantalon bleu/noir. |
| | [zhuh shersh‿ū pōtalō bluh/nwa] |
| **Do you have this shirt** | **Vous avez cette chemise** [vooz‿avay set shuhmeez] |
| in white, too | en blanc aussi [ō blō ohsee] |
| in another colour? | dans une autre couleur? [dōz‿oon‿otr kooluhr] |
| I don't like this colour. | Cette couleur ne me plaît pas |
| | [set kooluhr nuh muh play pa] |
| This colour is too light/dark. | Cette couleur est trop claire/trop foncée. |
| | [set kooluhr‿ay tro klair/tro fōsay] |

### Colours and patterns

| | | | |
|---|---|---|---|
| **beige** beige [bayzh] | | **light pink** rose pâle [rohz pahl] | |
| **black** noir,-e [nwa] | | **patterned** fantaisie [fōtaysee] | |
| **blue** bleu,-e [bluh] | | **pink** rose [rohz] | |
| **brown** marron [marō] | | **plain-coloured** uni [oonee] | |
| **checked** à carreaux [a karoh] | | **purple** lilas [leela] | |
| **colourful** multicolore [multeekolor] | | **red** rouge [roozh] | |
| **dark** foncé,-e [fōsay] | | **striped** rayé,-e [rayay] | |
| **green** vert,-e [vair,-t] | | **turqoise** turquoise [toorkwaz] | |
| **grey** gris,-e [gree,-z] | | **white** blanc (blanche) [blō (blōsh)] | |
| **light** clair,-e [klair] | | **yellow** jaune [zhohn] | |

*Train à Grande Vitesse (TGV), the French high-speed train*

# Getting Around

## Customs formalities

\* Votre passeport! [votr paspor]
\* Votre permis de conduire!
[votr pairmee duh kõdweer]

Your passport!
Your driving licence!

**I am**
    on holiday
    on a business trip.

**Je suis** [zhuh swee]
    en vacances [õ vakõs]
    en voyage d'affaires. [õ vwayazh dafair]

\* Vous avez quelque chose à
déclarer? [vooz‿avay kelk
shos‿a dayklaray]

Do you have anything to declare?

**No,**
    I have nothing to declare

    I have only a few presents.

**Non,** [nõ]
    je n'ai rien à déclarer
    [zhuh nay ryãn‿a dayklaray]
    je n'ai que quelques cadeaux.
    [zhuh nay kuh kelk kadoh]

Do I have to pay duty on this?

Il faut le déclarer, ça? [eel foh luh dayklaray sa]

\* Ouvrez la valise, s'il vous
plaît! [oovray la valeez seel voo
play]

Open the suitcase, please!

**Can I**
    call the British embassy

    call my consulate?

**Puis-je** [pweezhuh]
    faire appel à l'ambassade britannique
    [fair‿apel‿a lõbasad‿õglay]
    faire appel à mon consulat?
    [fair‿apel‿a mõ kõsoola]

## Asking directions

### How do I get

| | |
|---|---|
| to ... | **Comment est-ce que j'arrive** [komõ esk_zhareev] à ... [a] |
| on to the motorway | à l'autoroute [a lohtoroot] |
| to the city centre | au centre ville [o sõtr veel] |
| to ... Square | à la place ... [a la plas] |
| to ... Street | à la rue ... [a la roo] |
| to the station/bus station | à la gare/à l'arrêt d'autobus [a la gar/a laray_dohtoboos] |
| to the airport/harbour? | à l'aéroport/au port? [a layropor/o por] |

| | |
|---|---|
| * Au carrefour [o karfoor] | At the crossroads |
| * Après les feux [apray lay fuh] | After the traffic lights |

| | |
|---|---|
| * **Après cinq cents mètres** [apray sã_sõ metr] | **After 500 metres** |
| * tournez à droite/à gauche [toornay a drwat/a gosh] | turn right/left |
| * continuez tout droit [kõteenooay too drwa] | go straight ahead |
| * faites demi-tour. [fayt duhmee toor] | turn around. |

| | |
|---|---|
| Is this the road to ...? | Est-ce la bonne route pour aller à ...? [ays la bon root poor_alay a] |
| How far is it to ...? | A quelle distance sommes-nous de ...? [a kel deestõs som noo duh] |
| Can you show me that on the map? | Pourriez-vous me le montrer sur la carte? [pooree-ay voo muh luh mõtray soor la kart] |

## Car, motorbike and bicycle hire

### I'd like to hire

| | |
|---|---|
| a car | **Je voudrais louer** [zhuh voodray loo-ay] une voiture [oon vwachoor] |
| a four-wheel drive | une voiture tout-terrain [oon vwachoor too tairõ] |
| a minibus | un minibus [ũ meeneeboos] |
| a camper van | un camping-car [ũ kõpeeng kar] |
| a motorbike | une moto [oon moto] |
| a moped/a motorised bicycle | un vélomoteur/une motocyclette [ũ vaylomotuhr/oon motoseeklet] |
| a scooter | un scooter [ũ skooter] |
| a bicycle/a mountainbike | une bicyclette/un VTT [oon beeseeklet/ũ vaytaytay] |
| for two days/one week | pour deux jours/une semaine [poor duh zhoor/oon suhmen] |
| from today/tomorrow | à partir d'aujourd'hui/de demain. [a parteer dozhoordwee/duh duhmã] |

### What do you charge

| | |
|---|---|
| per day/per week | **Quel est le tarif** [kel_ay luh tareef] à la journée/à la semaine [a la zhoornay/a la suhmen] |
| per kilometre? | au kilomètre parcouru? [oh keelometr parkooroo] |

| | |
|---|---|
| Is there a mileage charge? | Est-ce que le kilomètrage est limité? [eskuh luh keelometrazh‿ay leemeetay] |
| How much petrol is left in the tank? | Combien d'essence y a-t-il encore dans le réservoir? [kõbyã desõs ee‿yateel‿õkor dõ luh ruhsuhvwar] |
| What petrol does it take? | Quelle essence faut-il mettre? [kel‿esõs foht‿eel metr] |
| How much is the deposit? | A combien s'élève la caution? [a kõbyã selev la kohsyõ] |
| Does the vehicle have comprehensive insurance? | Le véhicule a une assurance tous risques? [luh vayeekool a oon‿asyorõs too reesk] |
| When do I have to be back by? | Jusqu'à quelle heure faut-il rendre le véhicule? [zhooska kel‿uhr foht‿eel rõdr luh vayeekool] |

## Parking

| | |
|---|---|
| Can I park here? | Je peux garer ma voiture ici? [zhuh puh garay ma vwachoor‿eesee] |
| **Is there a . . . near here?** | **Est-ce qu'il y a . . . près d'ici?** [eskeelya . . . pray deesee] |
| a (supervised) car park | un parking (gardé) [ũ parkeeng (garday)] |
| a multi-storey car park/a garage? | un parking à étages/un parking souterrain [ũ parkeeng a aytazh/ũ parkeeng sootairã] |
| **How much is it** | **Quel est le tarif du parking** [kel‿ay luh tareef doo parking] |
| per hour | à l'heure [a luhr] |
| per day | à la journée [a la zhoornay] |
| per night? | par nuit? [par nwee] |

## Traffic signs

**Allumez vos phares** turn your head-lights on
**Attention** Caution
**Autoroute (payante)** motorway (subject to toll)
**Bouchon** traffic jam
**Chantier** road works
**Contrôle de radar** radar control
**Danger** danger
**Déviation** diversion
**Embouteillage** traffic jam
**Horodateur** parking meter
**Impasse** cul-de-sac
**Interdiction de dépasser** no overtaking
**Interdiction de stationner** no parking

**Parking à étages** multi-storey car park
**Parking souterrain** underground car park
**Piste cyclable** cycle path
**Poids lourds** heavy loads
**Ralentissez** reduce speed
**Sens unique** one-way street
**Serrez à droite** keep right
**Sortie de véhicules** exit
**Station de péage** toll booth
**Virage dangereux** dangerous bend
**Voie de dégagement** bypass
**Voie réservée aux véhicules lents** slow lane
**Vous n'avez pas la priorité** give way

# Petrol

| | |
|---|---|
| Where's the nearest petrol station, please? | Où est la station-service la plus proche? [oo ay la stasyō sairvees la ploo prosh] |

**Fill her up, please./20 litres of . . . please.**
  regular
  super
  diesel
    unleaded.

**Faites le plein/Vingt litres, s'il vous plaît**
[fayt luh plã/vã leetr seel voo play]
  de l'ordinaire [duh lordeenair]
  du super [doo soopair]
  du gasole [doo gazol]
    sans plomb. [sõ plõ]

I'd like half a litre of oil, please.

Je voudrais un demi-litre d'huile.
[zhuh voodrays‿ũ duhmee leetr dweel]

# Breakdown, accident

I have a flat tyre
I've had an accident.

J'ai un pneu à plat [zhay ũ pnuh a pla]
J'ai eu un accident. [zhay oo ũn‿aksseedō]

My car's broken down.

Ma voiture est en panne. [ma vwachoor ayt‿õ pan]

**Could you give me a lift**

  to the nearest petrol station

  to a garage?

**S'il vous plaît, emmenez-moi**
[seel voo play ōmnay mwa]
  à la prochaine station-service
  [a la proshen stasyō sairvees]
  à un garage. [a ũ garazh]

**Could you**
  tow my car away
  help me (push the car)
  help me jump-start my car

  lend me some petrol

  lend me your jack
  send for a breakdown truck

  call the police/fire brigade

  call an ambulance
  call a doctor?

**Pourriez-vous** [pooree-ay voo]
  me remorquer [muh ruhmorkay]
  m'aider (à pousser) [mayday (a poosay)]
  m'aider à démarrer avec votre batterie
  [mayday a daymaray avek votr batree]
  me donner un peu d'essence
  [muh donay ũ puh desõs]
  me prêter votre cric [muh pretay votr kreek]
  appeler le service de dépannage
  [apuhlay luh sairvees duh daypanazh]
  appeler la police/les pompiers
  [apuhlay la polees/lay pōpyay]
  appeler une ambulance [apuhlay oon‿ōbyoolōs]
  appeler un médecin? [apuhlay ũ medsã]

Are you injured?
Nobody is injured.
Somebody is (seriously) injured.

Vous êtes blessé? [vooz‿et blesay]
Personne n'est blessé. [pairson nay blesay]
Quelqu'un est (gravement) blessé.
[kelkũn‿ay (gravmō) blesay]

**Give me . . ., please.**

  your name and address

  your insurance number

**Donnez-moi, s'il vous plaît,**
[donay mwa seel voo play]
  votre nom et adresse
  [votr nõ ay adres]
  votre numéro d'assurance.
  [votr noomairo dasyorōs]

# Cars, motorbikes, bicycles

| | |
|---|---|
| automatic car | la voiture automatique [la vwachoor‿ohtomateek] |
| battery | la batterie [la batuhree] |
| brake | le frein [luh frã] |
| bicycle tyre | le pneu [luh pnuh] |
| car | la voiture [la vwachoor] |
| car key | la clé de la voiture [la klay duh la vwachoor] |
| catalytic converter | le catalyseur [luh kataleesuhr] |
| chain | la chaîne [la shen] |
| child seat | le siège-auto [luh see-ezh‿ohto] |
| clutch | l'embrayage (m) [löbray-azh] |
| engine | le moteur [luh motuhr] |
| exhaust | le pot d'échappement [luh po dayshapmö] |
| fan belt | la courroie [la koorwa] |
| first-aid kit | la trousse de secours [la troos duh suhkoor] |
| fuse | le fusible [luh foozeebl] |
| hand brake | le frein à main [luh frã a mã] |
| headlights | le phare avant [luh far‿avö] |
| helmet | le casque [luh kask] |
| horn | le klaxon [luh klaxö] |
| lights | le phare [luh far] |
| puncture repair kit | les nécessaires (m) de réparations [le nesesair duh rayparasyö] |
| pump | la pompe à air [la pöp‿a ayr] |
| radiator | le radiateur [luh radee-atuhr] |
| rear light | le feu arrière [luh fuh aree-air] |
| repair | la réparation [la rayparasyö] |
| screw | la vis [la vees] |
| screwdriver | le tournevis [luh toornuhvees] |
| seat belt | la ceinture de sécurité [la sãchoor duh saykyooreetay] |
| short circuit | le court-circuit [luh koor seerkwee] |
| spare part | la pièce de rechange [la pee-es duh ruhshözh] |
| spare tyre | la roue de secours [la roo duh suhkoor] |
| spark plugs | les bougies (f) [lay boozhee] |
| starter | le démarreur [luh daymaruhr] |
| steering | la direction [la deereksyö] |
| tools | les outils (m) [layz‿ootee] |
| tow rope | le cable de dépannage [luh kabl duh daypanazh] |
| tyre | le pneu [luh pnuh] |
| valve | la soupape [la soopap] |
| warning triangle | le triangle de présignalation [luh treeögl duh prayseenyalasyö] |
| windscreen wiper | l'essuie-glace (m) [leswee glas] |

was/You were/He was
driving too fast

driving too close.

Je/Vous/Il [zhuh/voo/eel]
roulais/rouliez/roulait trop vite
[roolay/roolee-ay/roolay tro veet]
me suis/vous êtes/s'est trop approché.
[muh swee/vooz_et/say trop_aproshay]

Did you witness the accident?

Vous êtes témoin de l'accident?
[vooz_et taymwä duh lakseedō]

Thank you very much for
your help.

Je vous remercie de votre aide.
[zhuh voo ruhmairsee duh votr_ayd]

## Garage

Is there a dealer ... near here?

Y a-t-il un concessionaire ... près d'ici?
[ee_yateel ü kōsesyonair pray deesee]

The engine
won't start
is losing oil
doesn't work properly.

Le moteur [luh motuhr]
ne démarre pas [nuh daymar pa]
perd de l'huile [pair duh lweel]
ne fonctionne pas bien. [nuh fōksyon pa byä]

The brakes don't work.

Les freins ne répondent pas bien.
[lay frä nuh raypōd pa byä]

The warning light is on.
The exhaust/radiator is
leaking/faulty.
How much will the repairs be?

Le témoin est allumé. [luh taymwä ayt_aloomay]
Le pot d'échappement/Le radiateur est percé/fuit.
[luh po dayshapmō/luh radeeatuhr ay pairsay/fooee]
La réparation va coûter combien?
[la rayparasyō va kootay kōbyä]

When will the car be ready?

Quand est-ce que la voiture sera prête?
[kōt_eskuh la vwachoor suhra pret]

## Hitchhiking

Are you going to ...?
Could you give me a lift?

Vous allez à ...? [vooz_alay a]
Pourriez-vous m'emmener?
[pooree-ay voo mōmnay]

I'd like to get out here, please!

Je voudrais descendre ici!
[zhuh voodray duhsōdr_eesee]

Thanks for the lift!

Merci de m'avoir emmené,-e!
[mairsee duh mavwar_ōmuhnay]

## Getting around by train and bus

Where's the station/
bus station, please?

Où est la gare/l'arrêt d'autobus, s'il vous plaît?
[oo ay la gar/laray dohtoboos seel voo play]

When's the next train to ...?

A quelle heure part le prochain train pour ...?
[a kel uhr par luh proshä trä poor]

Do I have to change?

Est-ce que je dois changer? [eskuh zhuh dwa
shōzhay]

Which platform does the train
leave from?

Le train part de quelle voie?
[luh trä par duh kel vwa]

When does the train/bus
arrive in ...?

A quelle heure est-ce que le train/le bus arrive
à ...? [a kel_uhr eskuh luh trä/luh boos_areev a]

## Signs

**Accès aux quais** access to the platforms
**Eau non-potable** not for drinking
**libre** vacant
**occupé** occupied
**Quai** platform
**Renseignements** information

**Signal d'alarme** emergency brake
**Sortie** exit
**Toilettes** toilets
**Voie** platform
**Voiture-couchette** couchette
**Wagon-lit** sleeper/sleeping car
**Wagon-restaurant** dining car

Is there a connection to ... in ...?

J'ai une correspondance à ... pour aller à ...?
[zhay oon korayspõdõs a ... poor_alay a]

How much is it?

Quel est le prix du billet?
[kel_ay luh pree doo beeyay]

Are there special rates for children?

Y a-t-il un tarif réduit pour enfants?
[ee_yateel_ũ tareef raydwee poor_õfõ]

**A ... ticket/tickets to ... , please.**
single/return
first-class/second-class

for two adults and two children.

**Un ticket/des tickets pour ... s'il vous plaît.**
[ũ teekay/day teekay poor ... seel vous play]
aller/aller-retour [alay/alay ruhtoor]
première/deuxième classe
[pruhmee-air/duhzee-em klas]
pour deux adultes et deux enfants.
[poor duhs_adoolt ay duhs_õfõ]

**I'd like to book ... on the two o'clock train/bus.**

**J'aimerais une réservation pour le train/bus de quatorze heures** [zhay_muhray oon raysairvasyõ poor luh trã/boos duh katorz_uhr]

to ...
a (window) seat
a non-smoker/smoker seat

a couchette
a sleeper.

pour ... [poor]
une place (côté fenêtre) [oon plas (kotay fuhnetr)]
une place non-fumeur/une place fumeur
[oon plas nõ foomuhr/oon plas foomuhr]
une couchette [oon kooshet]
une place en wagon-lit. [oon plas_õ vagõ lee]

**I'd like**
to take my bicycle with me.
to check in my luggage.

**Je voudrais** [zhuh voodray]
emporter ma bicyclette [õportay ma beeseeklet]
faire enregistrer mes bagages.
[fair_õruhzheestray may bagazh]

**Where can I find ... , please?**

the information desk

the left-luggage office

**S'il vous plaît, où est-ce que je trouve**
[seel voo play oo eskuh zhuh troov]
le guichet de renseignements
[luh geeshay duh rõsenyuhmõ]
la consigne des bagages
[la kõseenyuh day bagazh]

Is this the train/bus to ...?

Est-ce le train/bus pour ...?
[ays luh trã/boos poor]

Is this seat free, please?

Cette place est libre, s'il vous plaît?
[set plas_ay leebr seel voo play]

# Getting around by plane

**I'd like**
a flight to ...
for 1/2/4

on the...
one-way/return

economy class/first class.

to confirm a return flight
to cancel the flight/
change the booking.

**Je voudrais** [zhuh voodray]
un billet d'avion pour [ū beeyay davyō poor]
pour une/deux/quatre personne(s)
[poor‿oon/duh/katr pairson]
le ... [luh]
un billet aller/un billet aller-retour
[ū beeyay alay/ū beeyay alay ruhtoor]
classe touriste/première classe.
[klas tooreest/pruhmee-air klas]
confirmer un vol [kōfeermay ū vol]
annuler le vol/modifier mon billet d'avion.
[anoolay luh vol/modeefee-ay mō beeyay davyō]

**Where's**
Terminal 1/2/3

the ... desk

the information desk?

When does the plane from
... arrive?

**Où est** [oo ay]
le terminal numéro un/deux/trois
[luh tairmeenal noomairo ū/duh/trwa]
le guichet de la compagnie ...
[luh geeshay duh la kōpanyee]
le guichet des renseignements?
[luh geeshay day rōsenyuhmō]
A quelle heure atterrit l'avion venant de ...?
[a kel‿uhr ateree lavyō vuhnō duh]

**Are there any ... seats left?**

window/aisle

smoking/non-smoking

**Est-ce qu'il y a encore des places**
[eskeelya ōkor day plas]
côté fenêtre/côté couloir
[kotay fuhnetr/kotay koolwar]
pour fumeurs/non-fumeurs?
[poor foomuhr/nō foomuhr]

How much is the ticket?

Are there any special rates/
stand-by seats?
When do I have to be at the
airport?
How much is the airport tax?

Quel est le prix du billet?
[kel‿ay luh pree doo beeyay]
Y a-t il des tarifs spéciaux/des places stand-by?
[ee‿yateel day tareef spaysyoh/day plas stōd ba-ee]
A quelle heure a lieu l'enregistrement?
[a kel‿uhr a lyuh lōruhzheestruhmō]
La taxe d'aéroport, c'est combien? [la tax
dayropor say kōbyā]

My bag/my suitcase

has been damaged
is missing.

Mon sac/Ma valise
[mō sak/ma valees]
est abimé,-e [ayt‿abeemay]
a disparu. [a deesparoo]

# Getting around by boat

When does the next boat/(car)
ferry leave for ...?

How long does the crossing
take?

A quelle heure est le prochain bateau/
ferry pour ...?
[a kel‿uhr ay luh proshā batoh/feree poor]

La traversée dure combien de temps?
[la travairsay joor kōbyā duh tō]

**I'd like**
a ticket to ...

first class/tourist class

reclining seats
a single cabin

a double cabin

an outside/inside cabin.

**Je voudrais** [zhuh voodray]
un billet de bateau pour ...
[ũ beeyay duh batoh poor]
première classe/classe touristique
[pruhmee-air klas/klas tooreesteek]
des sièges inclinables [day see-ezh‿ãkleenabl]
une cabine pour une personne
[oon kabeen poor oon pairson]
une cabine pour deux personnes
[oon kabeen poor duh pairson]
une cabine extérieure/intérieure.
[oon kabeen extayreeuhr/ãtayreeuhr]

I'd like to take the car
with me.

When do I/we have to be
on board?
When do we arrive at ...?

How long are we stopping?

Je voudrais emmener ma voiture.
[zhuh voodrays‿õmnay ma vwachoor]

A quelle heure faut-il être à bord?
[a kel‿uhr foht‿eel‿etr‿a bor]
Quand ferons-nous escale à ...?
[kõ fuhrõ noo eskal a]

L'escale durera combien de temps?
[leskal jooruhra kõbyã duh tõ]

# Public transport

## Bus, tram and underground

Is there a bus to ...?

How long does it take?

Y a-t-il un bus pour ...?
[ee‿yateel‿ũ boos poor]
Le trajet dure combien de temps?
[luh trazhay joor kõbyã duh tõ]

**Exuse me, where's**
the nearest bus stop

the nearest tram stop

the nearest underground
station?

**Où est ... s'il vous plaît.** [oo ay ... seel voo play]
l'arrêt d'autobus le plus proche
[laray dohtoboos luh ploo prosh]
l'arrêt de tram le plus proche
[laray duh tram luh ploo prosh]
la station de métro la plus proche?
[la stasyõ duh metro la ploo prosh]

**... goes to ...?**
Which bus
Which tram
Which tube

**... va à ...?** [va a]
Quel bus [kel boos]
Quel tram [kel tram]
Quel métro [kel metro]

When does the last bus/
the last train leave?

A quelle heure est-ce que le dernier bus/
le dernier tram part? [a kel‿uhr eskuh luh
dairnyay boos/luh dairnyay tram par]

Which line must I take?

How many stops is it?

Does this bus/this tram go
to...?

Quelle direction faut-il prendre?
[kel deereksyõ foht‿eel prõdr]
Il y a combien d'arrêts?
[eel‿ee a kõbyã daray]
Est-ce le bon bus/le bon tram pour aller à ...?
[ays luh bõ boos/luh bõ tram poor‿alay a]

## Le métro

The underground railway network in Paris is known as **le métro** [luh metro]. Only two other French cities, Marseille and Lyon, have a similar system. There are two signs that you need to understand. **Sortie**, a word that you will see in many public places, means exit and, if you follow signs marked **Correspondance**, you will eventually come to a connecting line. On the way to the platform, passengers must have their ticket stamped. Failure to do so could result in a fine, so look out for the machine and the accompanying sign which reads **N'oubliez pas de composter votre billet!**

| | |
|---|---|
| **Where do I have to** | **Où est-ce qu'il faut** [oo eskeel foh] |
| get off | descendre [duhsõdr] |
| change for ... | changer pour aller à ... [shõzhay poor‿alay a] |
| change | changer [shõzhay] |
| to get to the station | pour aller à la gare [poor‿alay a la gar] |
| to get to the airport | pour aller à l'aéroport [poor‿alay a la-ayropor] |
| to get to the ... Hotel | pour aller à l'hôtel ... [poor‿alay a lohtel) |
| to get to the city centre? | pour aller au centre? [poor‿alay o sõtr] |

Could you tell me when I have to get off, please.
Dites-moi quand je devrai descendre, s'il vous plaît.
[deet mwa kõ zhuh duhvray duhsõdr seel voo play]

A ticket to ..., please.
Un ticket pour ..., s'il vous plaît.
[ũ teekay poor ... seel voo play]

Are there day tickets?
Y a-t-il un abonnement d'un jour?
[ee‿yateel‿ũn‿abonmõ dũ zhoor]

I would like a multiple
-journey ticket.
Je voudrais un carnet. [zhuh voodrays‿ũ karnay]

How much is it to ...?
Quel est le prix pour aller à ...?
[kel‿ay luh pree poor‿alay a]

Could you stop here, please!
Arrêtez-vous ici, s'il vous plaît!
[aretay vooz‿eesee seel voo play]

### Taxi

Where's the nearest taxi rank?
Où est la station de taxi la plus proche?
[oo ay la stasyõ duh taxee la ploo prosh]

**Can you take me ..., please?**
**S'il vous plaît, conduisez-moi**
[seel voo play kõdweesay mwa]

| | |
|---|---|
| to the station | à la gare [a la gar] |
| to the hotel | à l'hôtel [a lohtel] |
| to the airport | à l'aéroport [a layropor] · |
| to the centre of town | au centre ville [o sõtr veel] |

How much is it to ...?
Quel est le tarif pour aller à ...
[kel‿ay luh tareef poor‿alay a]

Could you switch on the meter, please?
Mettez le taxamètre en marche, s'il vous plaît.
[metay luh taxametr‿õ marsh seel voo play]

Could you stop here, please.
Arrêtez-vous ici, s'il vous plaît.
[aretay vooz‿eesee seel voo play]

That's for you!
Voilà pour vous! [vwala poor voo]

31

*Many palatial hotels were built on the Côte d'Azur at the end of the 19th century*

# Accommodation

## Hotel and guesthouse

**Where can I find**
a good/cheap hotel

guesthouse
close to the beach
in the centre of town
in a quiet location?

**Y a-t-il ici** [ee‿yateel‿eesee]
un bon hôtel/un hôtel pas trop cher
[ũ bon‿ohtel/ũn‿ohtel pa tro shair]
une pension[oon põsyõ]
près de la plage [pray duh la plazh]
dans le centre [dõ luh sõtr]
dans un quartier tranquille?
[dõs‿ũ kartee-ay trõkeel]

Where is the ... hotel/
guesthouse?

Où est l'hôtel/la pension...?
[oo ay lohtel/la põsyõ]

### At the reception desk

I have a reservation.

My name is ...

J'ai réservé une chambre.
[zhay raysairvay oon shõbr]
Je m'appelle ... [zhuh mapel]

**Have you got any vacancies**

for 1 night
for 1 week
for 1/3 weeks?

**Vous avez encore une chambre**
[vooz‿avayz‿ãkor‿oon schãbr]
pour une nuit [poor‿oon nwee]
pour une semaine [poor‿oon suhmen]/pour
deux/trois semaines? [poor duh/trwa suhmen]

* Désolé, on est complet.
[desolay õn‿ay kõplay]
* Nous aurons une chambre
libre à partir du ... [nooz‿orõ
oon shõbr leebr‿a parteer doo]

I'm afraid we're fully booked.

There's a vacancy from ...

**I'd like/We'd like**

**Je voudrais/Nous voudrions**
[zhuh voodray/noo voodreeõ]

a room with a shower

une chambre avec douche
[oon shõbr‿avek doosh]

a single room

une chambre pour une personne
[oon shõbr poor‿oon pairson]

a double room

une chambre pour deux personnes
[oon shõbr poor duh pairson]

a room with twin beds

une chambre à deux lits
[oon shõbr‿a duh lee]

a room with a large
double bed
  with a bath and toilet
  with a balcony
  with a cot

une chambre avec un grand lit
[oon shõbr‿avek‿ũ grõ lee]
  avec salle de bains [avek sal duh bã]
  avec balcon [avek balkõ]
  avec un lit d'enfant [avek‿ũ lee dõfõ]

facing the beach/at the
front.

qui donne sur la plage/qui donne sur la rue.
[kee don syor la plazh/kee don syor la roo]

**How much is the room**

**Quel est le prix de la chambre**
[kel‿ay luh pree duh la shõbr]

per person
per night
per week
  with/without breakfast

par personne [par pairson]
par nuit [par nwee]
par semaine [par suhmen]
  avec/sans petit déjeuner
  [avek/sõ puhtee dayzhuhnay]

with half board
with full board

en demi-pension [õ duhmee põsyõ]
en pension complète
[õ põsyõ kõplet]

for children?

pour enfants? [poor‿õfõ]

## From multi-star luxury to country inns

The word **hôtel** does not always mean what you would expect. Do not enter the **hôtel de ville** and ask if there are any rooms available. It is not the town hotel but the town hall and the office of the local mayor.

Most hotels encountered by travellers are part of an official classification system with five different categories. A hexagonal blue plate with a large white H next to the hotel entrance will indicate the number of stars awarded to the establishment, which in turn gives some idea of overnight rates and level of comfort offered.

The **Châteaux Hôtels de France** [shatoh ohtel de frõs] are old buildings, often country mansions which have been converted into hotels, while the **Relais de Campagne** [ruhlay duh kõpanyuh] group often consist of upmarket hotels set in a scenic countryside locations.

If you are looking for somewhere less expensive, then you will probably decide on **chambres d'hôte** [shõbr doht] (B&B), an **auberge** [ohbairzh] (country inn), a **Logis de France** [lozhee duh frõs] or a **Relais de Tourisme** [ruhlay duh tooreesm].

The last two hotel chains are well known for their regional cooking. A **pension** [põsyõ] (guesthouse) will usually be family-run and offer half-board or full-board accommodation.

Does the room have a television/telephone?

Y a-t-il un télévision/un téléphone dans la chambre?
[ee‿yateel‿ũ telayveesyõ/ũ telayfon dõ la shõbr]

I'd like to see the room.

Je voudrais voir la chambre.
[zhuh voodray vwar la shõbr]

This room is pretty.

La chambre est jolie. [la shõbr‿ay zholee]

I don't like this room.

La chambre ne me plaît pas.
[la shõbr nuh muh play pa]

Do you have another room?

Avez-vous une autre chambre?
[avay vooz‿oon‿ohtr shõbr]

Can I pay by cheque/credit card?

Puis-je payer avec chèque/une carte de crédit?
[pweezhuh payay avek shek/oon kart duh kraydee]

**Do you have**
a car park
a (supervised) garage
a safe
a swimming-pool
a sauna
a private beach?

**Avez-vous** [avay voo]
un parking [ũ parkeeng]
un garage (surveillé) [ũ garazh (suhrvayay)]
un coffre-fort [ũ kofr for]
une piscine [oon peeseen]
un sauna [ũ sohna]
une plage privée? [oon plazh preevay]

**Where is**
the breakfast room/
the dining room?

**Où est** [oo ay]
la salle à manger?
[la sal‿a mõzhay]

**What time is**
breakfast
lunch
dinner?

**A quelle heure servez-vous** [a kel‿uhr sairvay voo]
le petit déjeuner [luh puhtee dayzhuhnay]
le déjeuner [luh dayzhuhnay]
le dîner? [luh deenay]

▶ (Food and Drink, see page 40)

Would you wake me tomorrow morning at 7, please.

Réveillez-moi demain matin à sept heures, s'il vous plaît. [rayvayay mwa duhmã matã a set‿uhr seel voo play]

My key, please.

Ma clé, s'il vous plaît. [ma klay seel voo play]

Room number 10, please.

Chambre numéro dix, s'il vous plaît.
[shõbr noomairo dees seel voo play]

**Where can I**
change money
cash traveller's cheques

buy stamps/postcards

post a letter
make a phone call?

**Puis-je ... ici?** [pweezhuh ... eesee]
changer de l'argent [shõzhay duh larzhõ]
encaisser des chèques de voyage
[õkaysay day shek duh vwayazh]
acheter des timbres/des cartes postales
[ashuhtay day tãbr/day kart postal]
poster une lettre [postay oon letr]
téléphoner [telayfonay]

Can I make a phone call to England from my room?

Puis-je téléphoner en Angleterre de ma chambre?
[pweezhuh telayfonay õn‿õgltair duh ma shõbr]

Please put me through to the following number ...

S'il vous plaît, passez-moi le numéro ...
[seel voo play pasay mwa luh noomairo]

## Hotel Reservation by Fax

| | |
|---|---|
| Hôtel Colbert | Hôtel Colbert |
| F-75000 Paris | F-75000 Paris |
| FAX ... | FAX ... |
| Dear sir, | Mesdames, Messieurs |
| *I/We would like* to reserve a room from 1 to 10 May 2001 for *one/two persons*, if possible with shower and balcony. | *Je voudrais/Nous voudrions* réserver une chambre avec douche et balcon pour *une personne/deux personnes* pour la période du 1 au 10 mai 2001. |
| Please let *me/us* know the price for a *single/double* room with *breakfast/half-board* and then confirm *my/our* booking. | *Je vous serais très reconnaissant,-e/ Nous vous serions très reconnaissants* de bien vouloir *m'informer/nous informer* le plus vite possible des tarifs d'une chambre *avec petit déjeuner/en demi-pension.* |
| Best wishes | Dans l'attente de votre confirmation *je vous prie/nous vous prions* d'agréer, Mesdames et Messieurs, l'expression de *mes/nos* sentiments distingués. |

Are there any letters for me?
Y a-t-il du courrier pour moi?
[ee˰yateel doo kooryay poor mwa]

### Complaints

The room is dirty/too loud.
La chambre n'est pas propre/est trop bruyante.
[la shōbr nay pa propr/ay tro brooyōt]

There's no (hot) water.
Il n'y a pas d'eau (chaude). [eelnya pa doh (shohd)]

The toilet does not work.
Les toilettes ne fonctionnent pas.
[lay twalet nuh fōksyon pa]

### ... does not work.
The shower
The light
The heating

### ... ne fonctionne pas. [nuh fōksyon pa]
La douche [la doosh]
La lumière [la loomee-air]
Le chauffage [luh shohfazh]

### There is/are no
towels

hangers
toilet paper

### Il manque [eel mōk]
des serviettes de toilette
[day sairvee-et duh twalet]
des cintres. [day sātr]
du papier hygiénique [doo papee-ay eezheneek]

### Could we have
an (extra) blanket

an (extra) pillow?

### Nous avons besoin [nooz˰avō buhsā]
d'une couverture (supplémentaire)
[doon koovairchoor (sooplaymōtair)]
d'un oreiller (supplémentaire).
[dūn˰orayay (sooplaymōtair)]

I've lost the key to my room.  J'ai perdu la clé de ma chambre.
[zhay pairdoo la klay duh ma shōbr]

### Departure

I'm leaving/We're leaving tomorrow/today.  Je pars/Nous partons demain/aujourd'hui.
[zhuh par/noo partō duhmã/ozhoordwee]

I'd like my bill, please.  Préparez la note, s'il vous plaît.
[prayparay la not seel voo play]

Would you call me a taxi, please.  Appelez un taxi, s'il vous plaît.
[apuhlay ū taxee seel voo play]

It's been very nice here.  Nous avons eu un séjour très agréable ici.
[nooz␣avōz␣oo ū sayzhoor trayz␣agrayabl␣eesee]

Thank you very much.  Merci beaucoup. [mairsee bohkoo]

Good-bye.  Au revoir. [o ruhvwar]

# Holiday cottage and holiday flat

We're looking for  Nous cherchons [nu shairshō]

a holiday cottage  une maison de vacances
[oon mayzō duh vakōs]

a holiday flat  un appartement de vacances
[ūn␣apartuhmō duh vakōs]

a (quiet) holiday flat  un appartement (tranquille)
[ūn␣apartuhmō (trōkeel)]

for 2/4 people  pour deux/quatre personnes
[poor duh/katr pairson]

for 6 days/2 weeks.  pour six jours/deux semaines.
[poor see zhoor/duh smayn]

How much is the flat/cottage?  Quel est le prix de l'appartement/la maison?
[kel␣ay luh pree duh lapartuhmō/la maysō]

How many rooms does the cottage have?  Combien de chambres a la maison?
[kōbyā duh shābr␣a la mayzō]

Are there any additional costs?  Y a-t-il des frais supplémentaires?
[ee␣yateel day fray sooplaymōtair]

Are pets/dogs allowed?  On peut emporter des animaux/des chiens?
[ō puht␣ōportay days␣aneemoh/day shyā]

Do we have to clean it before we leave?  Il nous faut faire le nettoyage final?
[eel noo foh fair luh netwayazh feenal]

Where can I  Où est-ce qu'on peut [oo eskō puh]

go shopping  faire des courses [fair day koors]

make a phone call  téléphoner [telayfonay]

do the laundry?  faire la lessive? [fair la lehseev]

# Camping

Have you got room for  Est-ce que vous avez encore de la place pour
[eskuh vooz␣avay ākor duh la plas poor]

a tent  une tente [oon tōt]

a caravan  une caravane [oon karavan]

a camper van?  un camping-car? [ū kōpeeng kar]

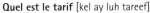

**What's the charge**
  for one person
  for a car
  for a camper van
  for a caravan
  for a tent?

**Quel est le tarif** [kel ay luh tareef]
  par personne [par pairson]
  par voiture [par vwachoor]
  par camping-car [par kõpeeng kar]
  par caravane [par karavan]
  par tente? [par tõt]

**Do you also rent out**
  caravans
  tents
  bungalows/cabins?

**Vous louez aussi** [voo loo-ay ohsee]
  des caravanes [day karavan]
  des tentes [day tõt]
  des bungalows/des cabanes?
  [day bũgalo/day kaban]

Where are the showers/
toilets?

Où sont les douches/W.C.?
[oo sõ lay doosh/vaysay]

**We need**
  an electric hookup
  a tap for water.

**Nous avons besoin** [nooz‿avõ buhwsã]
  d'électricité [delektreeseetay]
  d'un branchement d'eau. [dũ brõshmõ doh]

When is the gate locked at
night?
Is the camping site guarded at
night?

Quand est-ce que vous fermez la porte?
[kõt‿eskuh voo fairmay la port]
Le terrain est gardé pendant la nuit?
[luh tairã ay garday põdõ la nwee]

**Does the camping site have**

  a supermarket
  a restaurant
  public washing machines

  cool boxes
  a playground?

**Y a-t-il ... sur le terrain de camping?**
[ee‿yateel ... syor luh tairã duh kõpeeng]
  un supermarché [ũ soopairmarshay]
  un restaurant [ũ restorõ]
  des machines à laver à jetons
  [day masheen‿a lavay a zhuhtõ]
  des frigos [day freego]
  un terrain de jeux pour les enfants
  [ũ tairã duh zhuh poor les‿õfõ]

*If you want
comfort,
look for an
auberge in the
countryside*

## Youth hostel

| | |
|---|---|
| Is there a youth hostel around here? | Y a-t-il ici une auberge de jeunesse?<br>[ee‿yateel‿eesee oon‿ohbairzh duh zhuhness] |

**How much is it per night**    **Quel est le prix pour une nuit**
[kel‿ay luh pree poor‿oon nwee]

  per person (with breakfast)?    par personne (avec petit déjeuner)?
[par pairson (avek puhtee dayzhuhnay)]

We have a reservation.    Nous avons réservé.
[nooz‿avõ raysairvay]

Do you have a family room?    Avez-vous une chambre de famille?
[avay vooz‿oon shõbr duh famee]

## Accommodation

| | |
|---|---|
| adapter | l'adapteur *(m)* [ladaptuhr] |
| air conditioning | l'air *(m)* conditionné [lair kõdeesyonay] |
| apartment | l'appartement *(m)* [lapartuhmõ] |
| ashtray | le cendrier [luh sõdree-ay] |
| balcony | le balcon [luh balkõ] |
| bathtub | la baignoire [la baynwar] |
| bed | le lit [luh lee] |
| bedlinen | les draps [lay dra] |
| bill | la note [la not];<br>*(restaurant)* l'addition *(f)* [ladeesyõ] |
| bin | la poubelle [la poobel] |
| blanket | la couverture [la koovairchoor] |
| borrow | emprunter [õprütay]; |
| bottled gas | la bouteille de gaz [la butay duh gas] |
| camper van | le camping-car [luh kõpeeng kar] |
| caravan | la caravane [la karavan] |
| car park | le parking [luh parkeeng] |
| chamber maid | la femme de chambre [la fam duh schõbr] |
| clean *(vb)* | nettoyer [netwiyay] |
| coffee machine | la cafetière [la kafuhtyair] |
| coins | la monnaie [la monay] |
| cooker | la cuisinière [la kweeseenee-air] |
| cot | le lit d'enfant [luh lee dõfõ] |
| cutlery | le couvert [luh koovair] |
| dining room | la salle à manger [la sal‿a mõzhay] |
| drinking water | l'eau *(f)* potable [lo potabl] |
| electricity | le courant [luh koorõ] |
| extra costs | les frais *(m)* supplémentaires<br>[lay fray sooplemõtair] |
| family room | la chambre de famille [la schõbr duh famee] |
| fan | le ventilateur [luh võteelatuhr] |
| final cleaning | le nettoyage final [luh netwiyazh feenal] |
| garage | le garage [luh garazh] |

| | |
|---|---|
| I/We will stay for two days/ weeks. | Je resterai/Nous resterons deux jours/semaines. [zhuh ruhstuhray/noo ruhstuhrõ duh zhur/suhmen] |
| I need/I don't need bedlinen. | J'ai besoin/Je n'ai pas besoin de draps. [zhay buhswã/zhuh nay pa buhswã duh dra] |
| When is the front door locked? | La porte sera fermée à quelle heure? [la port suhra fairmay a kel‿uhr] |

**How far is it to**

**On met combien de temps pour aller**
[õ may kõbyã duh tõ poor‿alay]

| | |
|---|---|
| the beach | à la plage [a la plazh] |
| the town centre | au centre ville [o sõtr veel] |
| the station? | à la gare? [a la gar] |

| | |
|---|---|
| Is there a bus service to the centre of town? | Y a-t-il un autobus pour aller au centre ville? [ee‿yateel ũn‿ohtoboos poor‿alay oh sõtr veel] |

| | |
|---|---|
| guesthouse | la pension [la põsyõ] |
| hanger | le cintre [luh sãtr] |
| heating | le chauffage [luh schofazh] |
| hire charge | le tarif de location [luh tareef duh lokasyõ] |
| key | la clé [la klay] |
| kitchen | la cuisine [la kweeseen] |
| lend | prêter [pretay] |
| lift | l'ascenseur (m) [lasõsuhr] |
| light | la lumière [la loomee-air] |
| luggage | les bagages (m) [le bagazh] |
| pillow | l'oreiller (m) [lorayay] |
| pots and pans | les casseroles (f) [lay kasrol] |
| power point | la prise de courant [la preez duh koorõ] |
| radio | le radio [luh radyo] |
| reduction | la réduction [la raydooksyõ] |
| repair | réparer [rayparay] |
| rubbish | les ordures (f) [les‿ordoor] |
| safe | le coffre-fort [luh kofr for] |
| shower | la douche [la doosh] |
| sink | le lavabo [luh lavabo] |
| sleeping bag | le sac de couchage [luh sak duh kushazh] |
| soap | le savon [luh savõ] |
| sports ground | le terrain de sport [luh tairã duh spor] |
| tea towel | le torchon à vaisselle [luh torshõ a vaysel] |
| towel | la serviette de toilette [la sairvyayt duh twalet] |
| telephone | le téléphone [luh telayfon] |
| television | la télévision [la telayveesyõ] |
| toilet | les toilettes (f) [lay twalet] |
| toilet paper | le papier hygiénique [luh papee-ay eezheneek] |
| wash | laver [lavay] |
| washing machine | la machine à laver [la masheen‿a lavay] |
| water | l'eau (f) [loh] |
| water consumption | la consommation d'eau [la kõsomasyõ doh] |

*Drinking a black coffee at a pavement café is a mid-morning ritual*

# Food and Drink

### Is there ... around here?
a good restaurant/a reasonably cheap restaurant
a nice restaurant/
a typical restaurant
with regional/
international cuisine?

**Pourriez–vous m'indiquer** [pooree-ay voo mãdeekay]
un bon restaurant/un restaurant pas trop cher
[ũ bõ restohrõ/ũ restohrõ pa tro sher]
un restaurant sympa/un restaurant typique
[ũ restohrõ sãpa/ũ restohrõ teepeek]
avec cuisine régionale/internationale?
[avek kweeseen rayzhyonal/ãternasyonal]

### I'd like/We'd like

to have breakfast

to have lunch/dinner
a snack
just something to drink.

**Je voudrais/Nous voudrions**
[zhuh voodray/nu voodree-õ]
prendre le petit déjeuner
[prõdr luh puhtee dayzhuhnay]
déjeuner/dîner [dayzhuhnay/deenay]
prendre un repas rapide [prõdr_ũ ruhpa rapeed]
seulement boire quelque chose.
[suhlmõ bwar kelk shos]

### I'd like to reserve a table

for tonight
at 7/8 o'clock

for 4/6.

The name is ...

**Je voudrais réserver une table**
[zhuh voodray raysairvay oon tabl]
pour ce soir [poor suh swar]
à dix-neuf heures/vingt heures
[a dees_nuhf_uhr/vãt_uhr]
pour quatre/six personnes
[poor katr/see pairson]
au nom de ... [oh nõ duh]

I've reserved a table. The name is ...

J'ai réservé une table au nom de ...
[zhay raysairvay oon tabl_oh nõ duh]

A table for 2/4, please.

Une table pour deux/quatre personnes, s'il vous plaît. [oon tabl poor duh/katr pairson seel voo play]

40

| Is this table/seat free? | Cette table/place est libre? [set tabl/plas‿ay leebr] |
| Excuse me, where's the toilet? | Où sont les toilettes, s'il vous plaît? [oo sõ lay twalet seel voo play] |

## How to order

| Excuse me, please. | Monsieur, s'il vous plaît!/S'il vous plaît. [muhsyuh seel voo play/seel voo play] |
| Could I have the menu/menu of the day/wine list/list of ice creams, please. | La carte/Les plats du jour/La carte des vins/ La carte des glaces, s'il vous plaît. [la kart/lay pla doo zhoor/la kart duh vã/la kart day glas seel voo play] |
| What can you recommend? | Qu'est-ce que vous recommandez? [keskuh voo ruhkomõday] |

**I'll have** — **Je voudrais/Je prends** [zhuh voodray/zhuh prõ]

| soup | la soupe [la soop] |
| thick soup | le potage [luh potazh] |
| the dish of the day | le plat du jour [luh pla duh zhoor] |
| menu number 1/2 | le menu numéro un/deux [luh muhnoo noomairo ũ/duh] |
| this | ceci [suhsee] |
| as a starter/as the main course/for dessert. | comme hors-d'œuvre/plat principal/dessert. [kom‿or duhvr/pla prãseepal/daysair] |

| Do you have any regional specialities? | Quel sont les plats typiques? [kel sõ lay pla teepeek] |
| Could I have pasta/ rice instead of chips, please? | J'aimerais avoir des pâtes/du riz au lieu des frites. [zhaymuhrais‿avwar day pat/duh ree o lyuh day freet] |

**For the child/children ... , please.** — **Pour l'enfant/les enfants, s'il vous plaît** [poor lõfõ/les‿õfõ seel voo play]

| half portions | une demi-portion [oon duhmee porsyõ] |
| an extra plate | une assiette supplémentaire [oon asyet suhplaymõtair] |
| an extra set of cutlery. | un couvert supplémentaire. [ũ koovair suhplaymõtair] |

| Do you have a vegetarian dish? | Avez-vous un plat végétarien? [avay voo ũ pla vayzhaytaryã] |

**Is this dish** — **Ce plat est** [suh pla ay]

| hot/sweet/rich? | épicé/sucré/gras? [epeesay/suhkray/gra] |

| Do you sell wine by the carafe, too? | Vous avez aussi du vin en carafe? [vooz‿avay ohsee duh vã õ karaf] |

## Meal times

French people do not like to rush their lunch or evening meals. Breakfast, **petit déjeuner** [puhtee dayzhuhnay], in hotels and restaurants is usually served from 7 to 10am, lunch, **déjeuner** [luh dayzhuhnay], from noon to 2pm and the evening meal, **le dîner** [luh deenay], from 8 to 10pm.

## Bar – bistro – restaurant

A **bar** [bar] is a cross between a café and a pub. Every village usually has at least one, most holiday resorts have scores. Available at the bar, **le zinc** [luh zăk], the polished counter, will be not just a wide selection of alcoholic and non-alcoholic drinks, but also snacks, such as **un sandwich** [ŭ sŏweech] or a **croque-monsieur** [krok muhsyuh], a toasted cheese-and-ham sandwich.

The **brasserie** [brasree] was originally a place where only beer was served, but it has widened its repertoire to include other drinks and quick meals. The definition of **bistro** [beestro] is usually a small restaurant with a variety of "dishes of the day" on the menu, where the **patron** [patrŏ] himself cooks the meals. A **salon de thé** [salŏ duh tay] is a tea-room, not unlike an English café, while a **taverne** [tavairn] usually serves wine and snacks. If you do not have the time to sit and enjoy a meal in a traditional restaurant, look out for a **restaurant libre service** [restorŏ leebr sairvees], a self-service restaurant, or a basic **snack bar** [snak bar]. At motorway service stations, train stations and airports, you may see signs for a **restoroute** [restoroot]; a **buffet** [boofay] offers a quick cup of coffee and a bite to eat for travellers who are in a hurry.

You will probably not want to leave France without having sampled a meal in a proper French **restaurant** [restorŏ]. **Le déjeuner** [luh dayzhuhnay] (lunch) and **le dîner** [luh deenay] (evening meal) are served at set times. The menu will usually consist of a range of fixed-price meals with a varying number of courses and choices.

**To drink, I'd like/we'd like**

a glass of
a quarter of a litre of
(half) a bottle of red wine/white wine.

Thank you, that's all.

**Could I have . . ., please?**

some more bread
another beer

Enjoy your meal!
Cheers!/Your health!

* Santé! [sŏtay]

Do you mind if I smoke?

**J'aimerais/Nous aimerions boire**
[zhaymuhray/nooz aymuhree-ŏ bwar]
un verre de [ŭ vair duh]
un quart de [ŭ kar duh]
une (demi-) bouteille de vin rouge/vin blanc.
[oon (duhmee) bootay duh vă roozh/vă blŏ]

Merci, c'est tout. [mairsee say too]

**Puis-je encore avoir**
[pweezh ŏkor avwar]
un peu de pain [ŭ puh duh pă]
une bière? [oon bee-air]

Bon appétit! [bon apetee]
A votre santé! [a votr sŏtay]

Cheers!

Vous permettez que je fume?
[voo pairmetay kuh zhuh foom]

## Complaints

That's not what I ordered.

Have you forgotten my food/my drink?

Ce n'est pas ce que j'ai commandé.
[suh nay pa skuh zhay komŏday]

Avez-vous oublié mon repas/ma boisson?
[avay vooz ooblee-ay mŏ ruhpa/ma bwasŏ]

**Could we have ..., please?**    **S'il vous plaît, apportez–nous encore**
[seel voo play aportay nooz ōkor]

some cutlery    un couvert [ū koovair]
another knife/fork    un couteau/une fourchette
[ū kootoh/oon foorshet]
another (tea) spoon    une (petite) cuillère [oon (puhteet) kweeyair]
another plate/glass    une assiette/un verre [oon asyet/ū vair]
oil and vinegar    du vinaigre et de l'huile
[duh veenegr ay duh lweel]
salt and pepper    du sel et du poivre [duh sel ay duh pwavr]
some napkins    des serviettes [day sairvee-et]
an ashtray.    un cendrier. [ū sōdree-ay]

**I'm sorry but**    **Désolé, mais** [desolay may]

the food is cold    le repas est froid [luh ruhpa ay frwa]
the meat is tough/not    la viande est dure/n'est pas assez cuite.
cooked through.    [la vee-ōd ay joor/nay pas asay kweet]

There seems to be a mistake in    Je crois qu'il y a une erreur dans l'addition.
the bill    [zhuh krwa keeleeya oon eruhr dō ladeesyō]
What is this, please?    Qu'est-ce que c'est? [keskuh say]
I didn't have that.    Je n'ai pas eu cela. [zhuh nay pas oo sla]

## Paying the bill

Could I have the bill, please.    L'addition, s'il vous plaît. [ladeesyō seel voo play]
All together, please.    Je payerai le tout. [zhuh payuhray luh too]
Separate bills, please.    Nous payerons chacun notre part.
[noo payuhrō shakū notr par]
Could I have a receipt, please?    Je voudrais avoir un reçu, s'il vous plaît.
[zhuh voodrayz avwar ū ruhsoo seel voo play]

* Vous avez aimé?    Did you enjoy it?
[voos avay aymay]

It was very good, thank you.    Merci, c'était très bon. [mairsee setay tray bō]
That's for you.    Voici pour vous. [vwasee poor voo]
Keep the change.    Gardez la monnaie. [garday la monay]

## A votre santé

Before a meal, many French people enjoy drinking **un apéritif** [ū apereeteef] perhaps while sitting at the restaurant bar. If you are with French hosts, it is common to toast your companions with **à votre santé** [a votr sōtay] or **à ta santé** [a ta sōtay], depending on how familarly you know them – use the latter if you know the person well. The response is **à la vôtre** [a la votr] or **à la tienne** [a la tee-en]. As a quality control, French wine is classified under several categories. **Vin de pays** [vā duh payee] is country wine, **vin de table** [vā duh tabl] is table wine and **vin délimité de qualité supérieure (V. D. Q. S.)** [vā dayleemeetay duh kaleetay sooperee-uhr] is wine of superior quality from regulated sources. **Vin appellation d'origine contrôlée (A.O.C.)** [vā dappelasyō doreezheen kōtrolay] – the best of all wines produced in France – is bottled by the growers themselves.

# Food

| | |
|---|---|
| **Petit déjeuner** | **Breakfast** |
| beurre [buhr] | butter |
| biscottes [beeskot] | rusk |
| cacao [kakow] | cocoa |
| café (noir) [kafay (nwar)] | (black) coffee |
|   au/sans lait [oh/sõ lay] |   with/without milk |
|   décaféiné [daykafayeenay] |   decaffeinated |
|   sucré/avec du sucre allégé |   with sugar/sweetener |
|   [sookray/avek doo sookr‿alayzhay] | |
| charcuterie [sharkootuhree] | cold meats |
| chocolat [shokola] | hot chocolate |
| confiture [kõfichoor] | jam |
| croissant [krwasõ] | croissant |
| fromage [fromazh] | cheese |
| jambon (cru/cuit) [zhõbõ (kroo/kwee)] | (smoked/cooked) ham |
| jus d'orange [zhoo dorõzh] | orange juice |
| lait (chaud/froid) [lay (shoh/frwa)] | (hot/cold) milk |
| miel [mee-el] | honey |
| muesli [moo-ayslee] | muesli |
| œuf à la coque [uhf‿a la kok] | soft-boiled egg |
| œuf brouillé [uhf brweeyay] | scrambled egg |
| œuf sur le plat [uhf syor luh pla] | fried egg |
| omelette [omlet] | omelette |
| pain [pã] | bread |
| pain complet [pã kõplay] | wholemeal bread |
| thé [tay] | tea |
|   au citron/au lait [oh seetrõ/oh lay] |   with lemon/with milk |
| tisane [teesan] | herbal tea |
| | |
| **Casse-croûte** | **Snacks** |
| croque-monsieur [krok muhsyuh] | ham-and-cheese toasties |
| frites [freet] | chips |
|   avec du ketchup/avec de la mayonnaise |   with ketchup/ |
|   [avek doo ketchup/avek duh la mayonez] |   with mayonnaise |
| hamburger [õboorgair] | burger |
| hot-dog [ot dog] | hot dog |
| omelette [omlet] | omelette |
| sandwich [sõweech] | sandwich |
|   au fromage [o fromazh] |   with cheese |
|   au jambon/au saucisson |   with ham/with French |
|   [oh zhõbõ/oh sohseesõ] |   salami |
| saucisses [sohsees] | sausages |
| | |
| **Hors-d'œuvre** | **Cold starters** |
| assiette de charcuterie [asee-et duh sharkootree] | cold meats |
| crudités [kroodeetay] | raw vegetables with dressing |
| hors-d'œuvre variés [or duhvr varee-ay] | mixed starters |
| salade aux fruits de mer | seafood salad |
| [salad oh frwee duh mair] | |
| salade niçoise [salad neeswas] | salad with eggs and tuna |

**Entrées**

cuisses de grenouilles [kwees duh gruhnooy] — frog legs
escargots [eskargo] — snails
quenelles de brochet [kuhnel duh broshay] — pike dumplings
quiche lorraine [keesh loren] — quiche with bacon
tarte à l'oignon [tart_a lonyõ] — onion tart
tomates farcies [tomat farsee] — stuffed tomatoes

**Soupes et potages**

bouillabaisse [boo-eeyabes] — fish soup
pot-au feu [pot_oh fuh] — meat-and-vegetable hot pot
potage du jour [potazh doo zhoor] — soup of the day
soupe à l'ail [soop_a laiy] — garlic soup
soupe à l'oignon [soop_a lonyõ] — onion soup
velouté d'asperges [vuhlootay daspairzh] — asparagus soup
velouté de tomates [vuhlootay duh tomat] — tomato soup
velouté de volailles [vuhlootay duh volaiy] — chicken soup

**Poissons et fruits de mer**

anchois [õshwa] — anchovies
brochet [broshay] — pike
cabillaud [kabeeyoh] — cod
calmars (frits) [kalmar (free)] — (deep-fried) squid
carpe (farcie) [karp (farsee)] — (stuffed) carp
crevettes [kruhvet] — prawns
crustacés [kroostasay] — shellfish
écrevisse [aykruhvees] — crayfish
hareng [arõ] — herring
homard [omar] — lobster
langouste [lõgoost] — spiny lobster
maquereau [makuhroh] — mackerel
moules [mool] — mussels
poisson [pwasõ] — fish
  au court-bouillon/au four/frit/grillé — boiled/baked/
  [oh koor booeeyõ/oh foor/free/greeyay] — deep fried/grilled
sardines [sardeen] — sardines
saumon [sohmõ] — salmon
  fumé/poché [foomay/poshay] — smoked/poached
thon [tõ] — tuna
truite [trweet] — trout

**Viande**

agneau [anyoh] — lamb
bifteck [beeftek] — steak
  saignant/à point/bien cuit — rare/medium-rare/well-done
  [sehnyõ/a pwã/byã kwee]
blanquette de veau [blõket duh voh] — veal casserole
bœuf [buhf] — beef
bœuf bourguignon [buhf borgeenyõ] — beef stew with red wine
cassoulet [kasoolay] — casserole of meat and beans
choucroute garnie — sauerkraut with sausages
[shookroot garnee] — and pork

| | |
|---|---|
| cochon de lait [koshõ duh lay] | suckling pig |
| côte de bœuf [kot duh buhf] | beef on the bone |
| escalope (panée) [eskalop (panay)] | (breaded) escalope |
| faux-filet [foh feelay] | sirloin |
| foie [fwa] | liver |
| gigot d'agneau [zheego danyoh] | leg of lamb |
| gigot à la bretonne | leg of lamb with beans |
| [zheego a la bruhton] | |
| mouton [mootõ] | mutton |
| porc [por] | pork |
| rognons [ronyõ] | kidneys |
| rôti [rotee] | roast meat |
| steak au poivre vert [stek‿oh pwavr vair] | steak with green pepper |
| | corns |
| tournedos [toornuhdo] | tournedos/fillet |
| tripes [treep] | tripe (offal) |
| veau [voh] | veal |
| viande hachée [vee-õd ashay] | minced meat |

**Volaille/Gibier**

**Poultry/game**

| | |
|---|---|
| caille [kaiy] | quail |
| canard [kanar] | duck |
| (selle de) chevreuil [(sel duh) shevruhy] | (saddle of) venison |
| coq [kok] | chicken |
| dinde [dãd] | turkey |
| faisan [fuhsõ] | pheasant |
| lapin [lapõ] | rabbit |
| lièvre [lee-evr] | hare |
| oie [wa] | goose |
| perdrix [pairdree] | partridge |
| pigeon [peezhõ] | pigeon |
| pintade [pãtad] | guinea fowl |
| poulet [poolay] | chicken |
| sanglier [sõglee-ay] | wild boar |

**Garnitures**

**Side dishes**

| | |
|---|---|
| frites [freet] | chips |
| nouilles [nooy] | pasta |
| pain [pã] | bread |
| pommes dauphines [pom dofeen] | potatoes au gratin |
| pommes de terre (sautées/à l'anglaise) | (roast/boiled) potatoes |
| [pom duh tair (sotay/a lõglez)] | |
| riz [ree] | rice |

**Salades et légumes**

**Salads and vegetables**

| | |
|---|---|
| ail [aiy] | garlic |
| artichaut [arteeshoh] | artichoke |
| asperges [aspairzh] | asparagus |
| aubergine (farcie) [ohbairzheen (farsee)] | (stuffed) aubergine |
| bette [bet] | swiss chard |
| carottes [karot] | carrots |
| céleri [sayluhree] | celery |

| | |
|---|---|
| champignons [shŏpeenyŏ] | mushrooms |
| champignons de Paris [shŏpeenyŏ duh paree] | button mushrooms |
| chou [shoo] | cabbage |
| choux de Bruxelles [shoo duh brooxel] | Brussels sprouts |
| chou-fleur [shoo fluhr] | cauliflower |
| concombre [kŏkŏbr] | cucumber |
| courgettes [koorzhet] | courgettes |
| épinards [aypeenar] | spinach |
| fenouil [fuhnooy] | fennel |
| haricots (verts/blancs) [areeko (vair/blŏ)] | beans (green/haricot) |
| laitue [laytoo] | lettuce |
| (épi de) maïs [(aypee duh) ma-ees)] | corn (on the cob) |
| oignon [onyŏ] | onion |
| piment [peemŏ] | chilli pepper |
| pois [pwa] | peas |
| poivron [pwavrŏ] | sweet pepper |
| salade (composée) [salad (kŏposay)] | (mixed) salad |
| tomate [tomat] | tomato |

## Fromages / Cheese

| | |
|---|---|
| fromage de brebis [fromazh duh bruhbee] | ewe's cheese |
| fromage de chèvre [fromazh duh shevr] | goat's cheeese |
| fromage frais [fromazh fray] | soft cheese |
| fromage râpé [fromazh rapay] | grated cheese |
| gruyère [grooyair] | type of hard cheese |
| munster [moonstair] | type of aromatic cheese |
| roquefort [rokfor] | type of blue cheese |
| tomme de Savoie [tom duh savwa] | type of soft cheese made of cow's milk |

## Desserts / Desserts

| | |
|---|---|
| chantilly [shŏteeyee] | whipped cream |
| crêpe (suzette) [krep (soozet)] | thin pancake (flambé) |
| flan [flŏ] | custard tart |
| fruits (de saison) [frwee (duh saysŏ)] | (seasonal) fruit |
| gâteau [gatoh] | cake |
| mousse au chocolat [moos_oh shokola] | chocolate mousse |
| sabayon [sabayŏ] | dessert made of wine, sugar and egg yolks |
| salade de fruits [salad duh frwee] | fruit salad |
| tarte aux framboises [tart_oh frŏbwas] | raspberry tart |
| tarte aux pommes [tart_o pom] | apple tart |
| tarte tatin [tart tatã] | upside-down apple pudding |

▶ (Fruit, see shopping page 62)

## Glaces / Ice cream

| | |
|---|---|
| café liégeois [kafay lee-ayzhwa] | iced coffee |
| coupe de fruits [koop duh frwee] | fruit sundae |
| glace panachée [glas panashay] | mixed ice cream |
| avec de la chantilly [avek duh la shŏteeyee] | with cream |

glace [glas]
  parfum banane [parfü banan]
  parfum chocolat [parfü shokola]
  parfum citron [parfü seetrõ]
  parfum fraise [parfü frez]
  parfum framboise [parfü frõbwaz]
  parfum noisette [parfü nwazet]
  parfum pistache [parfü peestash]
  parfum vanille [parfü vaneey]

ice cream
  banana
  chocolate
  lemon
  strawberry
  raspberry
  nut
  pistachio
  vanilla

## Drinks

**Boissons alcoolisées**
apéritif [apayreeteef]
bière [bee-air]
  à la pression [a la presyõ]
  blonde/brune [blõd/broon]
  sans alcool [sõs‿alkol]
champagne [shãpanyuh]
cidre [seedr]
cognac [konyak]
eau-de-vie [oh duh vee]
gin [dzheen]
liqueur [leekuhr]
porto [porto]
punch [püsh]
rhum [rom]
sherry [sheree]
vermouth [vairmoot]
vin [vã]
  blanc/rosé/rouge [blõ/rosay/roozh]
  brut/doux/léger [broot/doo/layzhay]
  demi-sec/sec [duhmee sek/sek]
vin chaud [vã shoh]
whisky [weeskee]
  soda/avec glaçons [soda/avek glasõ]

**Alcoholic drinks**
apéritif
beer
  draught
  lager/brown ale
  alcohol free
champagne
cider
brandy
schnaps
gin
liqueur
port
punch
rum
sherry
vermouth
wine
  white/rosé/red
  very dry/very sweet/sweet
  medium dry/dry
mulled wine
whisky
  soda/on the rocks

**Boissons fraîches**
citron (pressé) [seetrõ (presay)]

eau [oh]
eau minérale [oh meenairal]
  gazeuse [gasuhs]
  naturelle [nachoorel]
frappé [frapay]
jus d'orange [zhoo dorõzh]
jus de fruits [zhoo duh frwee]
limonade [leemonad]
tonic [toneek]

**Soft drinks**
(freshly squeezed)
  lemon juice
water
mineral water
  sparkling
  still
milk shake
orange juice
fruit juice
lemonade
tonic water

▶ (Hot drinks, see breakfast page 44)

*France is very proud of its art treasures such as those displayed in the Louvre*

# Sightseeing

## Tourist information

| | |
|---|---|
| **Is there** | **Y a-t-il ici** [ee‿yateel‿eesee] |
| a tourist office here | un syndicat d'initiative [ū sädeeka deeneesyateev] |
| an information office here | un bureau de renseignements [ū byoroh duh rösenyuhmö] |
| | |
| **Are there** | **Y a-t-il ici** [ee‿yateel‿eesee] |
| guided tours | des visites guidées [day veezeet geeday] |
| sightseeing tours of the city? | des tours de ville organisés? [day toor duh veel organeesay] |
| | |
| **Do you have** | **Avez-vous** [avay voo] |
| a street map | un plan de ville [ū plö duh veel] |
| a map of the city centre/ the area | un plan du centre de la ville/des alentours [ū plö doo sötr duh la veel/des‿alötoor] |
| a map of the underground | un plan de métro [ū plö duh metro] |
| brochures | des prospectus [day prospektoos] |
| a list of hotels | une liste des hôtels [oon leest des‿ohtel] |
| a list of restaurants | une liste des restaurants [oon leest day restohrö] |
| | |
| a programme of events | un programme des spectacles [ū program day spektakl] |
| for this week? | pour cette semaine? [poor set suhmen] |
| | |
| Could you book a room for me? | Vous pourriez me faire réserver une chambre? [voo pooree-ay muh fair raysairvay oon shöbr] |
| | |
| What are the places of interest around here? | Qu'est-ce qu'il y a d'intéressant à voir ici? [keskeelya dätairesö a vwar‿eesee] |

# Sightseeing

| | |
|---|---|
| abbey | l'abbaye *(f)* [labayee] |
| altar | l'autel *(m)* [lohtel] |
| ancient | antique [ōteek] |
| arena | l'arène *(f)* [laren] |
| art | l'art *(m)* [lar] |
| artist | l'artiste [larteest] |
| | |
| Baroque | baroque [barok] |
| botanical gardens | le jardin des plantes [luh zhardã day plõt] |
| bridge | le pont [luh põ] |
| building | le monument [luh monyoomõ]/ |
| | le bâtiment [luh bateemõ] |
| | |
| castle | le château [luh shatoh] |
| catacomb | les catacombes *(f)* [lay katakõb] |
| cathedral | la cathédrale [la kataydral] |
| cave | la grotte [la grot] |
| ceiling fresco | la fresque de plafond [la fresk duh plafõ] |
| century | le siècle [luh see-ekl] |
| cemetery | le cimetière [luh seemuhtee-air] |
| church | l'église *(f)* [legleez] |
| convent | le couvent [luh koovõ] |
| copy | la copie [la kopee] |
| court (yard) | la cour [la koor] |
| cross | la croix [la krwa] |
| | |
| decorative arts | les arts décoratifs [les_ar daykorateef] |
| drawing | le dessin [luh desã] |
| | |
| era | l'époque *(f)* [laypok] |
| exhibit | l'exponat *(m)* [lexpona] |
| excavations | les fouilles *(f)* [lay fooy] |
| | |
| forest | la forêt [la foray] |
| fortress | la forteresse [la fortuhres] |
| | |
| garden | le jardin [luh zhardã] |
| gate | la porte [la port] |
| gorge | la gorge [la gorzh] |
| Gothic | gothique [goteek] |
| | |
| history | l'histoire *(f)* [leestwar] |
| | |
| inscription | l'inscription *(f)* [lãskreepsyõ] |
| island | l'île *(f)* [leel] |
| | |
| lake | le lac [luh lak] |
| landscape | le paysage [luh payzazh] |
| lane | la ruelle [la roo-el] |
| | |
| market | le marché [luh marshay] |
| medieval | médiéval [medeeayval] |
| monastery | le monastère [luh monastair] |

| | |
|---|---|
| monument | le monument [luh monyoomõ] |
| mosque | la mosquée [la moskay] |
| mountain | le mont [luh mõ] |
| | |
| national park | le parc national [luh park nasyonal] |
| nature reserve | la zone de protection de la nature [la zon duh proteksyõ duh la nachoor] |
| | |
| opera house | l'opéra (m) [lopaira] |
| organ | l'orgue (m) [lorg] |
| original | l'original (m) [loreezheenal] |
| | |
| painting | la peinture [la pãchoor] |
| | le tableau [luh tabloh] |
| painter | le peintre [luh pãtr] |
| palace | le palais (luh palay), le château [luh shatoh] |
| panorama | le panorama [luh panorama] |
| park | le parc [luh park] |
| pedestrian precinct | la zone piétonne [la zon pee-ayton] |
| picture | l'image (f) [leemazh] |
| port | le port [luh por] |
| prehistoric | préhistorique [prayeestoreek] |
| public park | l'espace (m) vert [lespas vair] |
| | |
| ramparts | le rempart [luh rõpar] |
| remains | les vestiges (m) [lay vesteezh] |
| Renaissance | la renaissance [la ruhnaysõs] |
| restore | restaurer [restohray] |
| Romanesque | roman [romõ] |
| roof | le toit [luh twa] |
| ruin (s) | la ruine [la rooeen] |
| | |
| sculpture | la sculpture [la skoolpchoor] |
| sights | les curiosités (f) [lay kyoreeoseetay] |
| square | la place [la plas] |
| stained-glass window | le vitrail [luh veetry] |
| statue | la statue [la stachoo] |
| style | le style [luh steel] |
| synagogue | la synagogue [la seenagog] |
| | |
| temple | le temple [luh tõpl] |
| theatre | le théâtre [luh tayatr] |
| tomb | le tombeau [luh tõboh] |
| tower | la tour [la toor] |
| town hall | la mairie [la mairee] |
| traditions | l'usage (m) [loosazh] |
| | |
| valley | la vallée [la valay] |
| view | la vue [la voo] |
| vineyard | le vignoble [luh vinyobluh] |
| | |
| waterfall | la cascade [la kaskad] |
| wine tasting | la dégustation de vins [la dayguhstasyõ duh vã] |
| | |
| zoo | le jardin zoologique [luh zhardã zoolozheek] |

# Visiting the sights

**I'd like/We'd like to visit**

the cathedral/church
the palace/castle

**J'aimerais/Nous aimerions visiter**
[zhayuhmray/nooz aymuhree-ō veeseetay]
la cathédrale/l'église [la kataydral/legleez]
le palais/le château. [luh palay/luh shatoh]

What are the opening hours
of the exhibition/museum?

Quelles sont les heures d'ouvertures de
l'exposition/du musée? [kel sõ les uhr
doovairchoor duh lexposeesyõ/doo moosay]

Is there a guided tour in
English?
When does it start?

Est-ce qu'il y a une visite guidée en anglais?
[eskeelya oon veeseet geeday õn õglay]
La visite est à quelle heure?
[la veeseet ayt a kel uhr]

How much is it?
How long does the tour take?

La visite est à quel prix? [la veeseet ayt a kel pree]
La visite dure combien de temps?
[la veeseet joor kõbyä duh tõ]

1/2 ticket(s) for adults/
children, please.
Are there special rates for
children/students/senior
citizens?

Un/Deux billet(s) pour adultes/enfants, s'il vous
plaît. [ũ/duh beeyay poor adoolt/õfõ seel voo play]
Y a-t-il un tarif réduit pour enfants/étudiants/
le troisième âge? [ee yateel ũ tareef raydoo-ee
poor õfõ/aytoodyõ/luh trwazee-em azh]

* Fermé pour rénovation.
[fairmay poor raynovasyõ]
* Photographies interdites!
[fotografee ätairdeet]

Closed for renovation.

No cameras allowed!

Can I use my video camera?

Je peux filmer ici? [zhuh puh feelmay eesee]

Do you have a catalogue/
guide in English?

Vous avez un catalogue/guide en anglais?
[vooz avay ũ katalog/geed õn õglay]

# Excursions

How much is the excursion
to ... ?
Do we have to pay extra for
the meal/for admission
charges?
Two tickets for today's
exursion/tomorrow's
excursion/for the excursion at
10 o'clock to ..., please.
When/Where do we meet?

When do we get back?

Quel est le prix d'un tour à ...?
[kel ay luh pree dũ toor a]
Les repas/Les billets d'entrée sont en plus?
[lay ruhpa/lay beeyay dõtray sõt õ ploos]

S'il vous plaît, deux places pour l'excursion à
... aujourd'hui/demain/à dix heures.
[seel voo play duh plas poor lexkoorsyõ a ...
ozhurdwee/duhmã/a dees uhr]
Quand/Où est-ce qu'on se rencontre?
[kõ/oo esk õ suh rõkõtr]
Quand est-ce qu'on va retourner?
[kõt esk õ va ruhtoornay]

**Do we have**
time to go shopping?

Do we also visit ...?

**Aurons–nous** [ohrõ noo]
du temps pour faire des achats?
[doo tõ poor fair des asha]

Est-ce qu'on va aussi visiter ...?
[esk õ va osee veeseetay]

*Sailing is a popular pastime in France, both on the northern coastline and on the Mediterranean*

# Active Pursuits

## At the beach and the swimming pool

Is there ... around here?
  an open air/indoor
  swimming pool
  a place to hire boats?

**Y a-t-il ici** [ee‿yateel‿eesee]
  une piscine en plein air/une piscine couverte
  [oon peeseen‿õ plän‿air/oon peeseen koovairt]
  une location de barques? [oon lokasyõ duh bark]

How far is it to the beach?
When is low tide/high tide?

La plage est loin? [la plazh‿ay lwã]
La marée haute/La marée basse est à quelle
heure? [la maray oht/la maray bas ayt‿a kel‿uhr]

Is there a strong current?

Y a-t-il des courants dangereux?
[ee‿yateel day kurõ danzhuhruh]

Are there jellyfish/sea urchins
in the water?

Y a-t-il des méduses/des oursins dans l'eau?
[ee‿yateel day maydooz/dayz‿oorsã dõ loh]

I'd like/We'd like to hire

**Je voudrais/Nous voudrions louer**
[zhuh voodray/noo voodree-õ loo-ay]

  a pedal/motor/
  rowing/sailing boat

  un pédalo/un canot à moteur/une barque à
  rames/un voilier [ũ paydalo/ũ kano a motuhr/
  oon bark‿a ram/ũ vwalee-ay]

  a deckchair
  a surfboard
  a pair of water skis

  une chaise longue [oon shes lõg]
  une planche à voile [oon plõsh‿a vwal]
  des skis nautiques. [day skee nohteek]

How much is it
  per (half) hour
  per day
  per week?

**Quel est le tarif** [kel‿ay luh tareef]
  par (demi-)heure [par (duhmee) uhr]
  à la journée [a la zhoornay]
  à la semaine? [a la suhmen]

I'm a beginner/
I'm experienced.

Je suis débutant (débutante)/avancée (avancé).
[zhuh swee daybyootõ (daybyootõt)/avõsay]

53

## Danger signs

| | |
|---|---|
| Avertissement de tempête | storm warning |
| Baignade interdite! | No swimming! |
| dangereux | dangerous |
| Défense de sauter! | No jumping! |
| Interdit aux non-nageurs! | No non-swimmers! |
| Pour les nageurs seulement! | Swimmers only! |

**Are there ... around here?**
sailing courses/sailing schools
surfing courses
diving courses

**Y a-t-il ici** [ee‿yateel‿eesee]
des cours/des écoles de voile
[day koor/dayz‿aykol duh vwal]
des cours de surf [day koor duh surf]
des cours de plongée sous-marine?
[day koor duh plõzhay soomareen]

## Sports

**Is there ... around here?**
a place to hire bikes
a (crazy) golf course

a tennis court
an ice rink

**Y a-t-il ici** [ee‿yateel‿eesee]
des bicyclettes à louer [day beeseeklet‿a loo-ay]
un terrain de golf (miniature)
[ũ tairã duh golf (meenee-achoor)]
un court de tennis [ũ koor duh tennis]
une patinoire? [oon pateenwar]

**Where can I**
go canoeing
go bowling/go horse riding

play squash/table tennis/ tennis?

**Où est-ce qu'on peut** [oo esk‿õ puh]
faire du kajak [fair doo kiyak]
jouer aux quilles/faire du cheval
[zhoo-ay oh keey/fair doo shuhval]
jouer au squash/ping-pong/tennis?
[zhoo-ay oh squash/ping pong/tenees]

**Where can I take**

tennis lessons
skiing lessons
snowboarding lessons

**Où est-ce que je peux m'inscrire à**
[oo eskuh zhuh puh mãskreer‿a]
un cours de tennis [ũ koor duh tenees]
un cours de ski [ũ koor duh skee]
un cours de monoski? [ũ koor duh monoskee]

Is swimming/fishing allowed here?

On a le droit de pêcher/de se baigner ici?
[õn‿a luh drwa duh peshay/duh suh benyay eesee]

**I'd like/We'd like to hire**

cross-country skis/downhill skis
ice-skating boots
a tennis racket.

**Je voudrais/Nous voudrions louer**
[zhuh voodray/noo voodree-õ loo-ay]
des skis de fond/des skis de descente
[day skee duh fõ/day skee duh duhsõt]
des patins [day patã]
une raquette de tennis. [oon raket duh tenees]

I'd like a ski pass for one (half a) day/one week.

Je voudrais un forfait pour une (demi-)journée/ une semaine.
[zhuh voodrays‿ũ forfay poor‿oon (duhmee) zhoornay/oon suhmen]

Do you play chess? Vous jouez aux échecs? [voo zhoo-ays_ohs_ayshek]
Do you mind if I join in? Puis-je jouer avec vous? [pweezhuh zhoo-ay avek voo]

**I'd like/We'd like to see** **Je voudrais/Nous voudrions voir**
[zhuh voodray/noo voodree-ō vwar]

the tennis/football match le match de tennis/de football
[luh match duh tenees/duh footbol]

the competition la compétition [la kōpayteesyō]
the (cycle/ski) race la course (cycliste/de ski)
[la koors (seekleest/duh skee)]

the regatta. la régate. [la raygat]

When does the event start? Quand est-ce que le spectacle va commencer?
[kōt_eskuh luh spektakl va komōsay]

Where does it take place? Où est-ce qu'il aura lieu? [oo esk_eel_ohra lyuh]

## Active pursuits

aerobics l'aérobic [la-ayrobeek]
arm bands les brassards *(m)* [lay brasar]
badminton le badminton [luh badminton]
ball le ballon [luh balō]
basketball le basketball [luh basketbol]
bay la baie [la bay]
billiards le billard [luh beeyar]
changing rooms le vestiaire [luh vestee-air]
cross-country course la piste de fond [la peest duh fō]
cross-country skiing le ski de fond [luh skee duh fō]
danger of avalanches le danger d'avalanche [luh dōnzhay davalōsh]
diving equipment l'équipement *(m)* de plongée
[laykeepmō duh plōzhay]
flippers les palmes *(f)* [lay palm]
gymnastics la gymnastique [la zheemnasteek]
health club le centre d'activités sportives
[luh sōtr dakteeveetay sporteev]
horse le cheval [luh shuhval]
horse-riding la sortie à cheval [la sortee a shuhval]
jogging le jogging [luh zhogeeng]
playground le terrain de jeu [luh tairā duh zhuh]
pony le poney [luh ponay]
rubber dinghy le canot pneumatique [luh kano pnuhmateek]
sauna le sauna [luh sohna]
shell le coquillage [luh kokeeyazh]
sled la luge [la loozh]
snorkelling le snorkelling [luh snorkelleeng]
snow la neige [la nezh]
storm la tempête [la tōpet]
suntan lotion la crème solaire [la krem solair]
swimming pool la piscine [la peeseen]
volleyball le volleyball [luh volaybal]
wave la vague [la vag]

## Nature, environment, adventure

**We'd like**
  to go on a cycle tour
  to go trekking
  to go hiking

  to go trekking in the nature reserve
  to go trekking in the national park.

**Nous voudrions faire** [noo voodree-ō fair]
  un tour en vélo [ũ toor͜ō vaylo]
  une excursion pédestre [oon exkoorsyō paydestr]
  une promenade en montagne
  [oon promuhnad͜ō mōtanyuh]
  une promenade à travers la réserve
  [oon promuhnad͜a travair la raysairv]
  une promenade à travers le parc national.
  [oon promuhnad͜a travair luh park nasyonal]

**Do you have**
  a hiking map

  a map of cycle paths?

**Avez-vous une** [avay vooz͜oon]
  carte de randonnée pédestre
  [kart duh rōdonay paydestr]
  carte de randonnée cycliste?
  [kart duh rōdonay seekleest]

**Is the route**
  easy/difficult
  well marked?

Is the route suitable for

children?
How long will it take?

Is this the right way
to ...?
How far is it to ...?

**Le tour est** [luh toor͜ay]
  facile/difficile [faseel/deefeeseel]
  bien marqué? [byã markay]

Le tour convient aux enfants?
[luh toor kōvyã ohs͜ōfō]
On met combien de temps pour faire ce tour?
[ō may kōbyã duh tō poor fair suh toor]

Est-ce le bon chemin pour aller à ...?
[es luh bō shuhmã poor͜alay a]
..., c'est à combien de kilomètres?
[set͜a kōbyã duh keelometr]

## Courses

**I'd like to attend**
  a language course
  a cookery/painting course

  a theatre/dance
  workshop.

Are there still places
available?

Where does the course/
the seminar take place?
How many people are taking
part in the course?
How much is the course?

Do you have somebody to
look after the children?

I have/I don't have any
previous knowledge.

**Je voudrais m'inscrire à** [zhuh voodray mãskreer a]
  un cours de langues [ũ koor duh lōg]
  un cours de cuisine/de dessin
  [ũ koor duh kweeseen/duh desã]
  un cours de théâtre/de danse.
  [ũ koor duh tayatr/duh dōs]

Est-ce qu'il y a encore des places libres?
[eskeelya ōkor day plas leebr]

Où est-ce que le cours/le séminaire aura lieu?
[oo eskuh luh koor/luh semeenair ohra lyuh]
Il y a combien de participants?
[eelya kōbyã duh parteeseepō]
Combien est-ce qu'il me faudra payer pour le
cours? [kōbyã esk͜eel muh fodra payay poor luh koor]
Est-ce que les enfants seront pris en charge?
[eskuh layz͜ōfō suhrō prees͜ō sharzh]

J'ai des/Je n'ai pas de connaissances.
[zhay day/zhuh nay pa duh konaysōs]

# Entertainment

## Cinema, theatre, opera and concerts

What's on at the cinema today/tomorrow?

Qu'est-ce qu'on donne au cinéma aujourd'hui/demain?
[kesk‿ō don‿oh seenayma ozhoordwee/duhmā]

**Is the film**
dubbed
shown in the original version (with subtitles)?

**Le film est** [luh feelm‿ay]
doublé [dooblay]
en version originale (sous-titré)?
[ō vairsyō oreezheenal (sooteetray)]

**When does … start?**

**A quelle heure commence**
[a kel‿uhr komōs]

the show
the film/the concert
the matinée
the ballet performance

le spectacle [luh spektakl]
le film/le concert [luh feelm/luh kōsair]
la matinée [la mateenay]
la représentation de ballet
[la ruhpraysōtasyō duh balay]

the cabaret
the opera/operetta
the musical
the play
the ticket sale
   for the festival?

le cabaret [luh kabaray]
l'opéra (f)/l'opérette (f) [lopayra/lopayret]
le musical [luh moozeekal]
la pièce de théâtre [la pee-es duh tayatr]
la vente des billets [la vōt day beeyay]
   pour le festival? [poor luh festeeval]

**What's on**
tonight/tomorrow night
this weekend
at the theatre
at the opera

**Qu'est-ce qui sera joué** [keskee sra zhooay]
ce soir/demain soir [suh swar/duhmā swar]
ce week-end [suh week‿end]
au théâtre [oh tayatr]
à l'opéra? [a lopayra]

## At the theatre

| | |
|---|---|
| à droite | right |
| à gauche | left |
| au milieu | centre |
| Balcon | circle |
| Côté | aisle |
| Deuxième Balcon | upper circle |
| Entrée | entrance |
| Galerie | gallery |
| Loge | box |
| Orchestre | stalls |
| Place | seat |
| Premier Balcon | dress circle |
| Rang | row |
| Sortie de secours | emergency exit |
| Toilettes | toilets |

Where do I get tickets? Où est-ce qu'on peut acheter les billets?
[oo esk‿ŏ puh ashuhtay lay beeyay]

How much are they? A combien sont les places? [a kŏbyā sŏ lay plas]

Are there still tickets at the box office? Est-ce qu'il y aura encore des billets ce soir?
[eskeelyohra ŏkor day beeyay suh swar]

Are there special rates? Y a-t-il des billets de tarif réduit?
[ee‿yateel day beeyay duh tareef raydwee]

\* Complet. [kŏplay] Sold out.

**Two tickets/seats ..., please.** **S'il vous plaît, deux billets/places**
[seel voo play duh beeyay/plas]

  for the show   pour le spectacle [poor luh spektakl]
  for the concert   pour le concert [poor luh kŏsair]
    tonight/tomorrow night     ce soir/demain soir [suh swar/duhmā swar]
    at 8 o'clock     à vingt heures. [a vāt‿uhr]

What time does the show end? A quelle heure termine le spectacle?
[a kel‿uhr tairmeen luh spektakl]

I would like a programme, please. Je voudrais avoir un programme, s'il vous plaît.
[zhuh voodrays‿avwar ŭ program seel voo play]

Is there a cloakroom? Y a-t-il un vestiaire? [ee‿yateel‿ŭ vestee-air]

## Nightlife

**Is there ... around here?** **Y a-t-il ici** [ee‿yateel‿eesee]
  a discotheque   une discothèque [oon deeskotek]
  a dance hall   un dancing [ŭ dŏseeng]
  a (nice) pub   une (jolie) taverne [oon (zholee) tavairn]
  a bar   un bar [ŭ bar]
  a casino   un casino [ŭ kaseeno]
    with (live) music?     avec de la musique (animée par un orchestre)? [avek duh la moozeek‿(aneemay par‿ŭn‿orkestr)]

# Entertainment

| | |
|---|---|
| actor (actress) | l'acteur (l'actrice) [laktuhr (laktrees)] |
| band | l'orchestre *(m)* [lorkestr] |
| bar | le bar [luh bar] |
| bouncer | le chasseur [luh shasuhr] |
| box office | la caisse [la kes] |
| cabaret | le cabaret [luh kabaray] |
| chamber music | la musique de chambre [la mooseek duh shõbr] |
| choir | le chœur [luh kuhr] |
| comedy | la comédie [la komaydee] |
| concert | le concert [luh kõsair] |
| conductor | le chef d'orchestre [luh shef dorkestr] |
| circus | le cirque [luh seerk] |
| dance hall | le dancing [luh dõseeng] |
| dancer | le danseur (la danseuse) [luh dõsuhr (la dõsuhs)] |
| director | le metteur en scène [luh metuhr‿õ sen] |
| discotheque | la discothèque [la deeskotek] |
| folk concert | la soirée folklorique [la swaray folkloreek] |
| go out | sortir [sorteer] |
| interval | l'entracte *(m)* [lõtrakt] |
| jazz concert | le concert de jazz [luh kõsair duh zhas] |
| matinée | la matinée [la mateenay] |
| musical | le musical [luh moozeekal] |
| open-air theatre | la scène en plein air [la sen‿õ plen‿air] |
| opera glasses | les jumelles *(f)* de théâtre [le zhoomel duh tayatr] |
| orchestra | l'orchestre *(m)* [lorkestr] |
| performance | la représentation [la ruhpraysõtasyõ] |
| play | la pièce de théâtre [la pee-es duh tayahtruh] |
| pop music | la musique pop [la mooseek pop] |
| première | la première [la pruhmee-air] |
| presentation | la présentation [la praysõtasyõ] |
| programme | le programme [luh program] |
| show | le spectacle [luh spektakl] |
| singer | le chanteur (la chanteuse) [luh shõtuhr (la shõtuhs)] |
| stage | la scène [la sen] |
| stage set | les décors *(m)* [le dekor] |
| ticket | le billet d'entrée [luh beeyay dõtray] |

Is this seat free? — Cette place est libre? [set plas‿ay leebr]

Could I see the drinks list, please. — La carte des boissons, s'il vous plaît. [la kart day bwasõ seel voo play]

**Shall we** — **Aimeriez-vous** [aymuhree-ay voo]
  dance — danser [dõsay]
  have a drink — boire quelque chose [bwar kelk shos]
  go for a stroll? — faire une petite promenade? [fair‿oon puhteet promuhnad]

This one's on me. — Je vous invite. [zhuh vooz‿ãveet]

**Can I** — **Puis-je** [pweezhuh]
  walk with you — faire un bout de chemin avec vous [fair‿ŭ boo duh shuhmã avek voo]
  walk you home — vous raccompagner [voo rakõpanyay]
  walk you to the hotel? — vous accompagner jusqu'à l'hôtel? [vooz‿akõpanyay zhooska lohtel]

Would you like to come to my place? — Vous aimeriez encore venir chez moi? [vooz‿aymuhreeyay õkor vuhneer shay mwa]

Thank you very much for the nice evening. — Merci beaucoup pour cette agréable soirée. [mairsee bohkoo poor set‿agrayabl swaray]

Good-bye/ See you tomorrow! — Au revoir/A demain [oh ruhvwar/a duhmã]

# Festivals and events

**When does ... start?** — **A quelle heure commence** [a kel‿uhr komõs]
  the festival — la fête [la fet]
  the festival programme — le programme de la fête [luh program duh la fet]
  the (trade) fair — la foire [la fwar]
  the matinée — la matinée [la mateenay]
  the parade/procession — le cortège/la procession [luh kortezh/la prosesyõ]
  the show/performance — la présentation [la praysõtasyõ]
  the circus? — le spectacle du cirque? [luh spektakl doo seerk]

Where does the show take place? — Où est-ce que le spectacle aura lieu? [oo eskuh luh spektakl ohra lyuh]

How long will it last? — Combien de temps va-t-il durer? [kõbjã duh tõ vat‿eel jooray]

Is there an admission charge? — Faut-il payer une entrée? [foht‿eel payay oon‿õtray]

Where do I get/ How much are the tickets? — Où puis-je prendre/A quel prix sont les billets? [oo pweezhuh prõdr/a kel pree sõ lay beeyay]

*There are no vending machines in France, but cigarettes can be bought at bars tabacs.*

# Shopping

## General

| | |
|---|---|
| **Is there ... around here?** | **Y a-t-il près d'ici** [ee‿yateel pray deesee] |
| a bakery | une boulangerie [oon boolōzhuhree] |
| a food store | une épicerie [oon aypeesuhree] |
| a butcher's shop | une boucherie [oon booshuhree] |
| a supermarket | un supermarché? [ū soopairmarshay] |

\* **Vous désirez?** [voo dayzeeray] What would you like?
\* **Puis-je vous aider?** Can I help you?
[pweezh vooz‿ayday]

I'm just looking, thanks. J'aimerais seulement regarder un peu.
[zhaymuhray suhlmō ruhgarday ū puh]

| | |
|---|---|
| **I'd like ..., please.** | **Je voudrais** [zhuh voodray] |
| stamps | des timbres [day tābr] |
| suntan lotion | une crème solaire. [oon krem solair] |

How much is this? Cela coûte combien? [sla koot kōbyā]
That's (too) expensive. C'est (trop) cher. [say (tro) shair]
I (don't) like that. Cela (ne) me plaît (pas).
[suhla (nuh) muh play (pa)]
I'll take it. Je le prends. [zhuh luh prō]

| | |
|---|---|
| **Do you have** | **Vous avez** [vooz‿avay] |
| anything else | autre chose [otr shos] |
| anything cheaper | quelque chose de moins cher |
| | [kelk shos duh mwa shair] |
| anything larger/smaller? | quelque chose de plus grand/de plus petit? |
| | [kelk shos duh ploo grō/duh ploo puhtee] |

## Groceries

| | |
|---|---|
| baby food | les alimentations (f) pour bébés [layz_aleemõtasyõ poor bebay] |
| biscuits | les biscuits (m) [lay beeskwee] |
| cake | le gâteau [luh gato] |
| chocolate | le chocolat [luh shokola] |
| (without) colouring | (sans) colorants (m) [(sõ) kolorõ] |
| cream | la crème [la krem] |
| eggs | les œufs (m) [layz_uh] |
| flour | la farine [la fareen] |
| fruit | les fruits (m) [le frwee] |
| juice | le jus [luh zhoo] |
| ketchup | le ketchup [luh ketchup] |
| margarine | la margarine [la margareen] |
| mayonnaise | la mayonnaise [la mayonez] |
| meat | la viande [la veeõd] |
| milk (full-cream/ skimmed) | le lait (entier/ écrémé) [luh lay (õtyay/aykremay)] |
| mustard | la moutarde [la mootard] |
| nuts | les noix (f) [lay nwa] |
| oil | l'huile (m) [lweel] |
| pepper | le poivre [luh pwavr] |
| porridge oats | les flocons (m) d'avoine [lay flokõ davwan] |
| (without) preservatives | (sans) conservateurs (m) [(sõ) kõsairvatuhr] |
| rusk | la biscotte [la beeskot] |
| salt | le sel [luh sayl] |
| sausages | les saucisses (f) [lay sosees] |
| spices | les épices (f) [layz_aypees] |
| sugar | le sucre [luh sookr] |
| tinned food | les conserves (f) [lay kõsairv] |
| vegetables | les légumes (m) [lay laygoom] |
| vinegar | le vinaigre [luh veenegr] |

▶ (See also food, page 44)

## Fruit and vegetables

| | |
|---|---|
| apple | la pomme [la pom] |
| apricot | l'abricot (m) [labreeko] |
| artichoke | l'artichaut (m) [larteeshoh] |
| aubergine | l'aubergine (f) [lohbairzheen] |
| avocado | l'avocat (m) [lavoka] |

| | |
|---|---|
| banana | la banane [la banan] |
| basil | le basilic [luh baseeleek] |
| beans (green/haricot) | les haricots *(m)* (verts/blancs) [layz‿areeko (vairt/blõ)] |
| broccoli | le broccoli [luh brokolee] |
| cabbage | le chou [luh shoo] |
| carrots | les carottes *(f)* [lay karot] |
| cherries | les cerises *(f)* [lay suhrees] |
| chicory | la chicorée [la sheekoray] |
| chilli pepper | le piment [luh peemõ] |
| courgette | la courgette [la koorzhet] |
| cucumber | le concombre [luh kõkõbr] |
| dates | les dattes *(f)* [lay dat] |
| figs | les figues *(f)* [lay feeg] |
| garlic | l'ail *(m)* [laiy] |
| grapes (white/red) | les raisins *(m)* (blancs/noirs) [lay raysã [blõ/nwar]] |
| iceberg lettuce | la batavia [la batavya] |
| kiwi | le kiwi [luh keewee] |
| leek | le poireau [luh pwaroh] |
| lemon | le citron [luh seetrõ] |
| mandarin orange | la mandarine [la mõdareen] |
| mango | la mangue [la mõg] |
| melon | le melon [luh muhlõ] |
| nectarine | la nectarine [la nektareen] |
| olives | les olives *(f)* [layz‿oleev] |
| onion | l'oignon *(m)* [lonyõ] |
| orange | l'orange *(f)* [lorõzh] |
| parsley | le persil [luh pairsee] |
| peach | la pêche [la pesh] |
| peanuts | les cacahuètes *(f)* [lay kakowet] |
| pear | la poire [la pwar] |
| peas | les petits pois *(m)* [lay puhtee pwa] |
| pineapple | l'ananas *(m)* [lanana] |
| plum | la prune [la proon] |
| potatoes | les pommes *(f)* de terre [lay pom duh tair] |
| raspberries | les framboises *(f)* [lay frõbwas] |
| spinach | les épinards *(m)* [layz‿aypeenar] |
| strawberries | les fraises *(f)* [lay frez] |
| sweetcorn | le maïs [luh ma-ees] |
| sweet pepper | le poivron [luh pwavrõ] |
| tomato | la tomate [la tomat] |
| water melon | la pastèque [la pastek] |

## Fresh bread on Sunday?

You ate your last piece of bread on Saturday evening and are worried about Sunday breakfast. It's no problem. In France the bakeries or **boulangeries** [boolōzhuhree] open on Sunday mornings. But what to eat for breakfast on Monday may need some thought as many bakers close on this day.

| | |
|---|---|
| **Can I** | **Puis-je** [pweezhuh] |
| pay by cheque | payer avec un chèque [payay avek‿ū shek] |
| pay by traveller's cheque | payer avec un chèque de voyage [payay avek‿ū shek duh vwayazh] |
| pay by credit card | payer avec une carte de crédit [payay avayk‿oon kart duh kraydee] |
| exchange this? | l'échanger? [layshōzhay] |

* Et avec ça? [ay avek sa]  Anything else?

That's all, thanks.  Merci, c'est tout. [mairsee say too]
Can you pack it for me, please?  Pouvez-vous l'emballer? [poovay voo lōbalay]
Do you have a carrier bag?  Je peux avoir un sac? [zhuh puh avwar‿ū sak]

## Groceries

| | |
|---|---|
| **I'd like/Could I have . . ., please?** | **Je voudrais/Donnez-moi, s'il vous plaît** [zhuh voodray/donay mwa seel voo play] |
| a piece of . . . | un morceau de . . . [ū morsoh duh] |
| 100 grams of. . . | cent grammes de . . . [sō gram duh] |
| (half) a kilo of . . . | un (demi-)kilo de . . . [ū (duhmee) keelo duh] |
| a litre of . . . | un litre de . . . [ū leetr duh] |
| a tin/bottle of . . . | une boîte/une bouteille de . . . [oon bwat/oon bootay duh] |

Could I try some of this, please?  Je peux en déguster? [zhuh puh ō daygoostay]

* C'est un peu plus. Ça va? [set‿ū puh ploos sa va]  It's a bit over. Is that all right?

A bit more/less, please.  Un peu plus/moins, s'il vous plaît. [ū puh ploos/mwã seel voo play]

It's all right!  C'est bon! [say bō]

## Books, stationery and newspapers

| | |
|---|---|
| **Do you sell** | **Avez-vous** [avay voo] |
| English papers/magazines | des journaux anglais/des revues anglaises [day zhoornoh ōglay/day ruhvoo ōglayz] |
| postcards | des cartes postales [day kart postal] |
| English books | des livres en anglais [day leevr‿ōn‿ōglay] |
| glue/adhesive tape? | de la colle/du ruban adhésif? [duh la kol/doo roobō adayseef] |

**I'd like**
a map of ...

a street map
a travel guide
a hiking map

a French–English
dictionary.

**Je voudrais** [zhuh voodray]
une carte géographique de ...
[oon kart zhayografeek duh]
un plan de la ville [ũ plõ duh la veel]
un guide touristique [ũ geed tooreesteek]
une carte de randonnée pédestre
[oon kart duh rõdonay paydestr]
un dictionnaire français-anglais.
[ũ deeksyonair frõsay õglay]

**Do you sell**
stamps
writing paper
envelopes
pens/pencils?

**Avez-vous** [avay voo]
des timbres [day tãbr]
du papier à lettres [doo papee-ay a letr]
des enveloppes [des˽õvolop]
des stylos/des crayons?
[day steelo/day krayõ]

## Clothes and shoes

**I'm looking for**
a blouse/a shirt

a T-shirt
a pair of trousers/a skirt/
a dress
a sweater/a jacket
underwear/socks

a raincoat
a pair of shoes/a pair of
trainers
for ladies/men/
children.

**Je cherche** [zhuh shairsh]
un chemisier/une chemise
[ũ shuhmeezee-ay/oon shuhmeez]
un T-shirt [ũ teeshirt]
un pantalon/une jupe/une robe
[ũ põtalõ/oon zhoop/oon rob]
un pullover/une veste [ũ poolovair/oon vest]
des sous-vêtements *(m)*/des chaussettes *(f)*
[day soo vetmõ/day shoset]
un imperméable [ũn˽ãpairmayabl]
des chaussures *(f)*/des baskets *(m)*
[day shohsyoor/day basket]
pour dames/hommes/enfants.
[poor dam/om/õfõ]

65

| | |
|---|---|
| I take size 40. | Je porte du quarante. [zhuh port doo karõt] |
| I take size 39. | Je chausse du trente-neuf. [zhuh shos doo trõt nuhf] |
| Could I try this on? | Puis-je l'essayer? [pweezhuh⌣lesay-yay] |
| Do you have a mirror? | Où y a-t-il un miroir? [oo⌣yateel⌣ũ meerwar] |
| It fits nicely/It doesn't fit. | Cela (ne) va (pas) bien. [suhla (nuh) va (pa) byã] |
| I (don't) like this. | Cela (ne) me plaît (pas). [suhla (nuh) muh play (pa)] |
| I like/I don't like the colour. | J'aime/Je n'aime pas la couleur. [zhaym/zhuh naym pa la kooluhr] |
| I'll take it. | Je le prends. [zhuh luh prõ] |
| Do you have other models/colours? | Y a-t-il encore d'autres modèles/d'autres couleurs? [yateel⌣õkor dotr model/dotr kooluhr] |

**It is**
  too small/too big
  too long/too short
  too tight/too loose.

**C'est** [say]
  trop petit/trop grand [tro puhtee/tro grõ]
  trop long/trop court [tro lõ/tro koor]
  trop serré/trop large. [tro seray/tro larzh]

**Is this**
  real leather
  cotton/wool/silk/linen?

**Est-ce** [ays]
  du cuir véritable [doo kweer vereetabl]
  du coton/de la laine/de la soie/du lin? [doo kotõ/duh la len/duh la swa/doo lã]

## Laundry and dry cleaning

| | |
|---|---|
| I'd like to have these things cleaned/washed. | Je voudrais faire nettoyer/laver cela. [zhuh voodray fair netwiyay/lavay suhla] |
| How much is it? | Ça coûte combien? [sa koot kõbyã] |
| When can I pick it up? | Quand est-ce que je peux venir le chercher? [kõt⌣eskuh zhuh puh vuhneer luh shairshay] |

## Jewellery and watches

| | |
|---|---|
| My necklace/my watch/my alarm clock is broken. | Ma chaîne/Ma montre/Mon réveil est cassé,e. [ma shen/ma mõtr/mõ rayvay ay kasay] |
| Could you repair it? | Pourriez-vous réparer cela? [pooree-ay voo rayparay suhla] |

## Clothing and shoe sizes

When buying clothes and shoes in France, you will find that the system of sizing is different to that in Britain. With women's clothing, add 26 to your UK size, so a woman's 12 becomes a 38 in France. The difference in men's shirt sizes is 23, so a size 16 UK collar is 39 in France. With suits simply add 10 (UK40 is 50 in France). Shoe sizes are different too. Add 33 to your UK size (UK6 = 39).

## Clothes and shoes

| | |
|---|---|
| anorak | le blouson [luh bloosō] |
| belt | la ceinture [la sāchoor] |
| bikini | le bikini [luh beekeenee] |
| boots | les bottes *(f)* [lay bot] |
| boxer shorts | le calçon [luh kalsō] |
| bra | le soutien-gorge [luh sootyā gorzh] |
| cap | le bonnet [luh bonay] |
| gloves | les gants *(m)* [lay gō] |
| hat | le chapeau [luh shapoh] |
| knickers | le slip [luh slip] |
| sandals | les sandales *(f)* [lay sōdal] |
| scarf | le foulard [luh foolar] |
| sunhat | le chapeau de soleil [luh shapoh duh solay] |
| swimsuit/trunks | le maillot de bain [luh miyo duh bā] |
| tie | la cravate [la kravat] |
| tights | le collant [luh kolō] |
| tracksuit | le jogging [luh zhogeeng] |
| waistcoat | le gilet [luh zheelay] |

**I'd like**
  a new battery
  a bracelet
  a brooch/a ring
  some earrings.

**Je voudrais** [zhuh voodray]
  une autre pile [oon_otr peel]
  un bracelet [ū braslay]
  une broche/une bague [oon brosh/oon bag]
  des boucles d'oreilles. [day bookl doray]

**Is this**
  silver/gold
  silver-plated/gold-plated?

**Est-ce** [ays]
  de l'argent/de l'or [duh larzhō/duh lor]
  argenté/doré? [arzhōtay/doray]

## Electrical appliances and photography

**I'm looking for/I need**
  an adapter
  a battery
    for a walkman
    for a torch
    for a camera
    for a video camera
    for a radio.

**J'ai besoin** [zhay buhswā]
  d'un adapteur [dūn_adaptuhr]
  d'une pile [doon peel]
    pour un baladeur [poor ū baladuhr]
    pour une lampe de poche [poor oon lōp duh posh]
    pour un appareil photo [poor ūn_aparay foto]
    pour une caméra vidéo [poor oon kamera vidayo]
    pour un poste de radio. [poor ū post duh radyo]

**I'd like**
  a colour film
  a black and white film

  a slide film

    with 24/36 exposures.

**Je voudrais** [zhuh voodray]
  une pellicule couleur [oon peleekool kooluhr]
  une pellicule noir et blanc
  [oon peleekool nwar_ay blō]
  une pellicule pour diapos
  [oon peleekool poor deeapo]
    pour vingt-quatre/trente-six photos.
    [poor vā katr/trōt see foto]

**I'm looking for**
  a video casette

**Je cherche** [zhuh shairsh]
  une cassette vidéo (VHS)
  [oon kaset video (vay ash‿es)]

  a standard lens
  a wide-angle lens
  a telephoto lens
  a zoom lens.

  un objectif [ŭn‿obzhekteef]
  un grand angle [ŭ grŏd‿ŏgl]
  un téléobjectif [ŭ telayobzhekteef]
  un zoom. [ŭ zoom]

**Could you ..., please?**

**Pourriez-vous me**
[pooree-ay voo muh]

  put the film in the camera
  develop this film for me

  mettre la pellicule [metr la peleekool]
  développer cette pellicule
  [dayvelopay set peleekool]

  do prints
    9 by 13

    gloss
    matt

  faire les épreuves [fair layz‿aypruhv]
    format neuf-treize
    [forma nuhf trez]
    brillant [doo breeyŏ]
    mat? [mat]

Do you do passport photos?

Vous faites des photos d'identité?
[voo fayt day foto deedŏteetay]

When will the prints be ready?

Quand les photos seront-elles prêtes?
[kŏ lay foto suhrŏt‿el pret]

**... doesn't work.**

**... ne fonctionne pas bien.**
[nuh fŏksyon pa byŏ]

  My camera
  My flash
  My video camera

  Mon appareil photo [mon aparay foto]
  Mon flash [mŏ flash]
  Ma caméra vidéo [ma kamera video]

Could you have a look at it?/Can you repair it?

Pourriez-vous regarder/le réparer?
[pooree-ay voo ruhgarday/luh rayparay]

When can I pick it up?

Quand est-ce que je peux venir le chercher?
[kŏt‿eskuh zhuh puh vuhneer luh shairshay]

## Souvenirs and arts and crafts

**I'm looking for**
  a souvenir
  folk costumes

**Je cherche** [zhuh shairsh]
  un souvenir [ŭ soovuhneer]
  des vêtements folkloriques
  [day vetmŏ folkloreek]

  ceramics
  art
    modern/antique/
    folk
  leather goods
  jewellery.

  de la céramique [duh la sayrameek]
  des objets d'art [des‿obzhay dar]
    moderne/antique/folklorique
    [modairn/ŏteek/folkloreek]
  de la maroquinerie [duh la marokeenuhree]
  des bijoux. [day beezhoo]

**What's typical of**

**Qu'est-ce qui est typique pour**
[keskee‿ay teepeek poor]

  this town
  this area
  this country?

  cette ville [set veel]
  cette région [set rayzhyŏ]
  ce pays? [suh payee]

**Is this**
  handmade
  genuine
  antique
  local artisan work?

**Est-ce** [ays]
  fait à la main [fayt‿a la mã]
  véritable [vayreetabl]
  antique [õteek]
  de l'artisanat d'art [duh larteezana dar]
  de la région? [duh la rayzhyõ]

# Optician

My glasses are broken.

J'ai cassé mes lunettes. [zhay kasay may loonet]

Can you repair them/let me have a replacement pair?

Pourriez-vous les réparer/m'en donner d'autres?
[pooree-ay voo lay rayparay/mõ donay dotr]

When can I pick up the glasses?

Quand est-ce que je peux venir chercher les lunettes?
[kõt‿eskuh zhuh puh vuhneer shairshay lay loonet]

I'm shortsighted/longsighted.

Je suis myope/presbyte.
[zhuh swee mee-op/presbeet]

**I have**
  lost my glasses
  lost my contact lens

  ... diopters in the right/left eye.

**J'ai** [zhay]
  perdu mes lunettes [pairdoo may loonet]
  perdu un verre de contact.
  [pairdoo ũ vair duh kõtakt]
  à droite/à gauche ... dixième.
  [a drwat/a gohsh ... deezee-em]

**I need**
  a pair of sunglasses
  a spectacle case
  a pair of binoculars
  cleansing-/rinsing solution for contact lenses

  for hard/soft contact lenses.

**J'ai besoin** [zhay buhswã]
  de lunettes de soleil [duh loonet duh solay]
  d'un étui à lunettes [dũ‿aytwee a loonet]
  de jumelles [duh zhoomel]
  d'un liquide pour nettoyer/tremper les verres de contact [dũ leekeed poor netwayay/trõpay lay vair duh kõtakt]
  pour des verres de contact durs/souples.
  [poor day vair duh kõtakt joor/soopl]

# Chemist

**I'd like**
  some plasters
  some tissues

  a hand/skin creme

  a suntan lotion with protection factor 6/12
  an after-sun lotion

  a shampoo
    for normal/dry/greasy hair

    for dandruff.

**Je voudrais** [zhuh voodray]
  des sparadraps [day sparadra]
  des mouchoirs en papier
  [day mooshwar‿ũ papee-ay]
  une crème pour les mains/la peau
  [oon krem poor lay mã/la poh]
  une crème solaire indice six/douze
  [oon krem solair ãdees sees/dooz]
  une crème après-soleil
  [oon krem apray solay]
  un shampooing [ũ shõpwã]
    pour cheveux normaux/secs/gras
    [poor shuhvuh normoh/sek/gra]
    anti-pelliculaire. [õtee peleekoolair]

# Tobacconist

| | |
|---|---|
| . . .,please. | ...s'il vous plaît. [... seel voo play] |
| A packet/carton of cigarettes | un paquet/une cartouche de cigarettes [ũ pakay/oon kartoosh duh seegaret] |
| with/without filters. | avec/sans filtre. [avek/sõ feeltr] |
| A packet of pipe tobacco | du tabac pour la pipe [doo taba poor la peep] |
| A box of matches | des allumettes [dayz‿aloomet] |
| A lighter | un briquet. [ũ breekay] |

# Chemist

| | |
|---|---|
| after-shave lotion | la lotion après-rasage [la losyõ apray rasazh] |
| baby powder | la poudre pour le bébé [la poodr poor luh baybay] |
| baby's bottle | le biberon [luh beebuhrõ] |
| body lotion | la lotion de toilette [la losyõ duh twalet] |
| brush | la brosse [la bros] |
| condom | le préservatif [luh prayzairvateef] |
| comb | le peigne [luh penyuh] |
| cotton wool | le coton [luh kotõ] |
| deodorant | le déodorant [luh dayodorõ] |
| dummy | la sucette [la sooset] |
| elastic hairband | l'élastique (m) pour cheveux [laylasteek poor shuhvuh] |
| hairspray | la laque [la lak] |
| insect repellent | la crème anti-moustique [la krem õteemoosteek] |
| lip salve | la pommade pour les lèvres [la pomad poor lay levr] |
| mirror | le miroir [luh meerwar] |
| nail file | la lime à ongles [la leem‿a õgl] |
| nail scissors | les ciseaux (m) à ongles [lay seezoh a õgl] |
| nail varnish | le vernis à ongles [luh vairnee a õgl] |
| nappies | les langes (m) [lay lõzh] |
| perfume | le parfum [luh parfũ] |
| razor-blade | la lame de rasoir [la lam duh raswar] |
| saftey pin | l'épingle (f) de sûreté [lepãgl duh syooruhtay] |
| sanitary towels | les serviettes (f) hygiéniques [lay sairvee-et eezheneek] |
| shampoo | le shampooing [le shõpoo-eeng] |
| shaving foam | la mousse à raser [la moos‿a rasay] |
| shower gel | le gel douche [luh zhel doosh] |
| soap | le savon [luh savõ] |
| styling gel | le gel cheveux [luh zhel shuhvuh] |
| tampons | les tampons (m) hygiéniques [le tõpõ eezheneek] |
| toothbrush | la brosse à dents [la bros‿a dõ] |
| toothpaste | le dentifrice [luh dõteefrees] |
| toilet paper | le papier hygiénique [luh papee-ay eezheneek] |
| tweezers | la pince à épiler [la pãs‿a aypeelay] |
| washing powder | le détergent [luh daytairzhõ] |
| washing-up liquid | le produit à vaisselle [luh prodwee a vaysel] |

To change your money go to a bureau de change or a cashpoint, which you can find in most towns

# Practical Information

## Medical assistance

### At the doctor's surgery

I need a doctor (urgently).

Je dois consulter un médecin (de toute urgence).
[zhuh dwa kõsooltay ũ maydsã (duh toot‿oorzhõs)]

Please call an ambulance.

Appelez une ambulance, s'il vous plaît.
[apuhlay oon‿õbyoolõs seel voo play]

### Where can I find a (English-speaking)

gynaecologist
paediatrician
dentist?

### Où est-ce que je peux trouver un … (qui parle anglais)?

[oo eskuh zhuh puh troovay ũ … (kee parl‿õglay)]

gynécologue [zheenaykolog]
pédiatre [paydee-atr]
dentiste [dõteest]

Can the doctor come here?

Le médecin pourrait venir?
[luh maydsã pooray vuhneer]

When are his surgery hours?

Quelles sont ses heures de consultation?
[kel sõ says‿uhr duh kõsooltasyõ]

Can I have an appointment immediately/wait here?
When can I come?

Je peux venir tout de suite/rester ici?
[zhuh puh vuhneer too duh sweet/restay eesee]
Quand est-ce que je peux venir?
[kõt‿eskuh zhuh puh vuhneer]

* Qu'est-ce qui ne va pas?
[keskee nuh va pa]

What can I do for you?

I feel sick/faint (all the time).

J'ai (très souvent) mal au cœur/des vertiges.
[zhay (tray soovõ) mal‿oh kuhr/day vairteezh]

I had a fall.

Je suis tombé,-e. [zhuh swee tõbay]

72

**I've got**
a cold
an allergy
diarrhoea
the flu
a cough
a headache
stomach-ache
earache
a sore throat
cystitis

heart trouble
a temperature.

**J'ai** [zhay]
pris froid [pree frwa]
une allergie [oon‿alairzhee]
la diarrhée [la dee-aray]
la grippe [la greep]
la toux [la too]
mal à la tête [mal‿a la tet]
mal au ventre [mal‿o võtr]
mal aux oreilles [mal‿ohz‿oray]
mal à la gorge [mal‿a la gorzh]
une affection de la vessie
[oon‿afeksyõ duh la vesee]
des troubles cardiaques [day troobl kardee-ak]
de la fièvre. [duh la fee-evr]

I've vomited.

J'ai vomi. [zhay vomee]

* Depuis quand avez-vous de la fièvre? [duhpwee kõt‿avay voo duh la fee-evr]

When did the fever start?

Two days ago.

Depuis deux jours. [duhpwee duh zhoor]

* Où est-ce que vous avez mal? [oo esk vooz‿avay mal]

Where does it hurt?

* Ce n'est rien de grave. [suh nay ryã duh grav]

It's nothing serious.

Is the leg/ the arm/ the finger broken?

La jambe/Le bras/Le doigt est cassé,-e?
[la zhõb/luh bra/luh dwa ay kasay]

I am allergic to penicillin.

Je ne supporte pas la pénicilline. [zhuh nuh sooport pa la payneeseeleen]

I've got digestion problems.

Je digère mal. [zhuh deezhair mal]

**I'm**
(3 months) pregnant
chronically ill.

**Je suis** [zhuh swee]
enceinte (de trois mois) [õsãt (duh trwa mwa)]
un malade chronique. [ũ malad kroneek]

I'm a diabetic.
I'm taking medication.

J'ai du diabète. [zhay doo deeabet]
Je prends régulièrement des médicaments.
[zhuh prõ raygoolee-airmõ day maydeekamõ]

## Directions for use of medicine

| | |
|---|---|
| à dissoudre dans l'eau | dissolve in water |
| à jeun | on an empty stomach |
| à sucer | dissolve on the tongue |
| avant/après les repas | before/after food |
| deux fois/trois fois par jour | twice/three times a day |
| pour usage externe | external |
| pour usage interne | internal |
| sans croquer | swallow whole |

**Could you**
  prescribe this for me

  prescribe something for . . ., please?

**Pourriez–vous** [pooree-ay voo]
  me prescrire cela
  [muh preskreer suhla]
  me prescrire quelque chose contre . . .?
  [muh preskreer kelk shos kõtr]

**At the dentist**

I've got (terrible) toothache/lost a filling.

J'ai (très) mal aux dents/perdu un plombage.
[zhay (tray) mal‿oh dõ/pairdoo ũ plõbazh]

**Could you**
  see me immediately

  give me something for the pain, please?

**Pourriez–vous** [pooree-ay voo]
  me faire un traitement tout de suite
  [muh fair‿ũ traytmõ too duh sweet]
  me donner un médicament pour calmer
  les douleurs? [muh donay ũ maydeekamõ poor
  kalmay lay dooluhr]

# Medical assistance

| | |
|---|---|
| AIDS | le SIDA [luh seeda] |
| allergy | l'allergie *(f)* [lalairzhee] |
| antibiotic | l'antibiotique *(m)* [lõteebyoteek] |
| appendicitis | l'appendicite *(f)* [lapõdeeseet] |
| aspirin | l'aspirine *(f)* [laspeereen] |
| bandage | les pansements *(m)* [lay põsmõ] |
| bleeding | l'hémorragie *(f)* [laymorazhee] |
| burn | la brûlure [la broolyoor] |
| certificate | l'attestation *(f)* [latestasyõ] |
| circulatory problems | les troubles *(m)* de la circulation |
| | [lay troobl duh la seerkyoolasyõ] |
| cold | le rhume [luh room] |
| cold sore | le bouton de fièvre |
| | [luh bootõ duh fee-evruh] |
| concussion | la commotion cérébrale [la komosyõ seraybral] |
| constipation | la constipation [la kõsteepasyõ] |
| cough | la toux [la too] |
| cough mixture | le sirop contre la toux [luh seero kõtr la too] |
| disinfectant | le désinfectant [luh daysãfektõ] |
| diabetes | le diabète [luh deeabet] |
| earache | mal aux oreilles [mal‿oz‿oray] |
| eardrops | les gouttes *(f)* pour les oreilles |
| | [lay goot poor layz‿oray] |
| eyedrops | le collyre liquide [luh koleer leekeed] |
| flu | la grippe [la greep] |
| fracture | la fracture [la frakchoor] |
| fungus infection | la mycose [la meekos] |
| gastroenteritis | les troubles *(m)* gastriques et intestinaux |
| | [lay troobl gastreek‿ay ãtesteenoh] |
| headaches | les maux de tête [le moh duh tet] |
| HIV-positive | séro-positif [sayro poseeteef] |

| | |
|---|---|
| Could you do a temporary repair on the tooth/the bridge/the crown. | S'il vous plaît, ne faites qu'un traitement provisoire de la dent/du bridge/de la couronne. [seel voo play nuh fayt kŭ traytmō proveeswar duh la dō/doo breedzh/duh la kooron] |
| Could you give me an/no injection, please. | Faites-moi une piqûre./Ne me faites pas de piqûre. [fayt mwa oon peekyoor/nuh muh fayt pa duh peekyoor] |
| Is it bad? | C'est grave? [say grav] |

### At the hospital

| | |
|---|---|
| Where is the nearest hospital? | Où est l'hôpital le plus proche? [oo ay lohpeetal luh ploo prosh] |

**Please call**  **S'il vous plaît, avertissez** [seel voo play avairteesay]
   Mr/Mrs ...     Monsieur/Madame ... [muhsyuh/madam]
   at the ... Hotel!     à l'hôtel ...! [a lohtel]

| | |
|---|---|
| infection | l'infection (f) [lãfeksyō] |
| infectious | contagieux (contagieuse) [kõtazhyuh (kõtazhyuhs)] |
| inflammation | l'inflammation (f) [lãflamasyō] |
| migraine | la migraine [la meegren] |
| ointment | la pommade [la pomad] |
| operation | l'opération (f) [loperasyō] |
| painkiller | le cachet contre la douleur [luh kashay kõtr la dooluhr] |
| plaster | le sparadrap [luh sparadra] |
| poisoning | l'empoisonnement (m) [lõpwasonuhmō] |
| pregnancy | la grossesse [la grosess] |
| pulled muscle | l'entorse (f) [lõtors] |
| pulled tendon | l'entorse (f) [lõtors] |
| pus | le pu [luh poo] |
| rash | les boutons (m) [lay bootō] |
| seasickness | le mal de mer [luh mal duh mair] |
| sleeping pills | le somnifère [somneefair] |
| snakebite | la morsure de serpent [la morsyoor duh sairpō] |
| sprained | foulé,-e [foolay] |
| sunstroke | l'insolation (f) [lãsolasyō] |
| sweat | la sueur [la soo-uhr] |
| temperature | la fièvre [la fee-evr] |
| tranquilizer | le calmant [luh kalmō] |
| travel sickness | le mal de transport [luh mal duh trõspor] |
| vaccinate | vacciner [vakseenay] |
| vaccination | la vaccination [la vakseenasyō] |
| virus | le virus [luh veeroos] |
| vomit (vb) | vomir [vomeer] |
| wound | la blessure [la blesyoor] |
| X-ray | radiographier [radeeografee-ay] |

Do you have private/two-bed rooms? — Avez-vous des chambres privées/des chambres à deux lits? [avay voo day shōbr preevay/day shōbr‿a duh lee]

What's the diagnosis? — Quel est le diagnostic? [kel‿ay luh deeagnosteek]

What kind of therapy is necessary? — Quel traitement est-ce qu'il faudra? [kel traytmō eskeel fohdra]

How long will I have to stay? — Combien de temps est-ce que je devrai rester? [kōbjã duh tō eskuh zhuh duhvray restay]

(When) can I get up? — (Quand) Est-ce que je pourrai me lever? [(kōt‿) eskuh zhuh pooray muh luhvay]

I feel (don't feel any) better. — Je (ne) vais (pas) mieux. [zhuh (nuh) vay (pa) myuh]

**I need** — **J'ai besoin** [zhay buhswã]

a painkiller — d'un médicament qui calme les douleurs [dū maydeekamō kee kalm lay dooluhr]

sleeping pills. — d'un soporifique. [dū soporeefeek]

Am I well enough to travel? — Je peux voyager? [zhuh puh vwayazhay]

**I'd like . . .** — **Je voudrais** [zhuh voodray]

to see the doctor — parler au docteur [parlay oh doktuhr]

to be discharged — sortir de l'hôpital [sorteer duh lohpeetal]

a medical report — avoir un diagnostic [avwar‿ū dee-agnosteek]

a certificate — avoir une attestation [avwar‿oon‿atestasyō]

for my medical insurance — pour ma caisse d'assurance-maladie [poor ma kays dasyoorōs maladee]

for my doctor. — pour mon médecin de famille. [poor mō maydsã duh famee]

**At the pharmacy**

I'm looking for a pharmacy. — Je cherche une pharmacie. [zhuh shairsh‿oon farmasee]

I have a prescription./ I don't have a prescription. — J'ai une ordonnance./Je n'ai pas d'ordonnance. [zhay oon‿ordonōs/zhuh nay pa dordonōs]

**I need** — **J'ai besoin** [zhay buhswã]

something for a cough/ a headache/ sunburn — de quelque chose contre la toux/ les maux de tête/le coup de soleil [duh kelk shos kōtr la too/lay moh duh tet/ luh koo duh solay]

for me — pour moi [poor mwa]

for adults/children. — pour adultes/pour enfants. [poor‿adoolt/poor‿ōfõ]

Is the medicine strong/weak? — Le remède est fort/doux? [luh ruhmed‿ay for/doo]

How many tablets/drops do I have to take? — Combien de comprimés/gouttes faut-il prendre? [kōbjã duh kōpreemay/goot foht‿eel prõdr]

**Could you give me . . ., please.** — **S'il vous plaît, donnez–moi** [seel voo play donay mwa]

a receipt/a copy of the prescription — une quittance/une copie de l'ordonnance. [oon keetōs/oon kopee duh lordonōs]

**76**

# Holidays and festivals

Is there a holiday/national holiday today?
Aujourd'hui est un jour férié/une fête nationale? [ozhoordwee ayt‿ū zhoor fayree-ay/oon fet nasyonal]

What's being celebrated today?
C'est quelle fête aujourd'hui? [say kel fet ozhoordwee]

Where are the most interesting processions/parades?
Où y a-t-il les plus belles processions/les plus beaux cortèges? [oo ee‿yateel lay ploo bel prosesyō/lay ploo boh kortezh]

When does the festival start?
Quand est-ce que la fête commence? [kŏt‿eskuh la fet komŏs]

How long will it take?
La fête va durer jusqu'à quelle heure? [la fet va jooray zhooska kel‿uhr]

Where does the festival take place?
Où est-ce que la fête aura lieu? [oo eskuh la fet ohra lyuh]

Do we need tickets?
On a besoin de billets? [ŏn‿a buhswã duh beeyay]

Where do we get tickets?
Où est-ce qu'on peut avoir des billets? [oo esk‿ŏ puht‿avwar day beeyay]

How much are the tickets?
Quel est le prix des billets? [kel‿ay luh pree day beeyay]

# Money matters

**Can I pay with ... here?**
(travellers') cheques

cheque card
credit card

**Puis-je payer avec** [pweezhuh payay avek]
des chèques (de voyage) [day shek (duh vwayazh)]
la carte de chèque [la kart duh shek]
la carte de crédit? [la kart duh kredee]

**Where's the nearest**
bank
bureau de change
post office
cash dispenser?

**Où y a-t-il ici** [oo yateel‿eesee]
une banque [oon bŏk]
un bureau de change [ū byooroh duh shōzh]
un bureau de poste [ū byooroh duh post]
un guichet automatique? [ū geeshay ohtomateek]

**Where can I**
change some money/
cheques/traveller's cheques ?

**Où est-ce que je peux** [oo eskuh zhuh puh]
changer de l'argent [shõzhay duh larzhõ]
encaisser des chèques/des chèques de voyage?
[õkaysay day shek/day shek duh vwayazh]

Can I have money transferred
here from my bank?

Est-ce que je peux faire ici un virement de mon
compté en banque? [eskuh zhuh puh fair eesee ũ
veermõ duh mõ compt õ bõk]

* Combien désirez-vous?
[kõbyã dayseeray voo]

How much do you want?

300 (Francs).

Trois cents (Francs). [twa sõ (frõ)]

What's the current exchange
rate/the maximum amount
per cheque?

Quel est le cours de change actuel/le montant
maximum par chèque?
[kel_ay luh koor duh shõzh_akchoo-el/luh mõtõ
maxeemuhm par shek]

I'd like to change 100 pounds
sterling/dollars (into francs).

Je voudrais changer cent livres sterling/dollars
(en Francs français).
[zhuh voodray shõzhay sõ leevr sterling/dollar
(õ frõ frõsay)]

Please give me
100-Franc notes/
some coins as well!

S'il vous plaît, donnez-moi des billets de cent
Francs/aussi de la monnaie.
[seel voo play donay mwa day beeyay duh sõ frõ/
ohsee duh la monay]

Can I use my credit card to
get cash?

Je peux avoir des espèces avec ma carte de
crédit? [zhuh puh avwar days_espes avek ma kart
duh kredee]

* Votre carte de chèque,
s'il vous plaît! [votr kart duh
schek seel voo play]
* Signez ici, s'il vous plaît!
[seenyay eesee seel voo play]

Can I see your cheque card, please?

Sign here, please!

Has my bank transfer/money
order arrived yet?

Mon virement bancaire/Mon mandat-poste est
arrivé? [mõ veermõ bõkair/mõ mõda post
ayt_areevay]

# Crime and police

Where's the nearest police
station?
Please call the police!

Où est le commissariat de police le plus proche?
[oo ay luh komeesaree-a duh polees luh ploo prosh]
Appelez la police, s'il vous plaît!
[apuhlay la polees seel voo play]

**I've been**
robbed
mugged on the road/
at the beach.

**On m'a** [õ ma]
volé [volay]
attaqué dans la rue/à la plage.
[atakay dõ la roo/a la plazh]

This man is
bothering/following me.
My car has been broken into.

Ce monsieur m'incommode/me poursuit.
[suh muhsyuh mãkomod/muh poorswee]
On a fracturé ma voiture.
[õn_a frakchooray ma vwachoor]

**... has been stolen!**
My passport
My car/bicycle

My wallet
My camera
My handbag
My cheques/
My cheque card
My watch

**On m'a volé** [õ ma volay]
mon passeport [mõ paspor]
ma voiture/ma bicyclette
[ma vwachoor/ma beeseeklet]
mon portefeuille [mõ portuhfuhee]
mon appareil photo [mon‿aparay foto]
mon sac à main [mõ sak‿a mã]
mes chèques/ma carte de chèque.
[may shek/ma kart duh shek]
ma montre! [ma mõtr]

**I'd like to report**
a theft/a fraud/a robbery

a rape.

**Je voudrais déclarer** [zhuh voodray dayklaray]
un vol/une escroquerie/un hold-up
[ẽ vol/oon‿eskrokree/ũ‿nold‿uhp]
un viol. [ũ vyol]

**I'd like to**
report an accident
speak to a lawyer/
call my embassy.

**Je voudrais** [zhuh voodray]
déclarer un accident [dayklaray ũn‿akseedõ]
parler à un avocat. [parlay a ũn‿avoka]
parler à l'ambassade. [parlay a lõbasad]

Does anyone here speak
English?

Y a-t-il quelqu'un qui parle anglais?
[ee‿yateel kelkũ kee parl‿õglay]

**I need**
an interpreter
a written document for
insurance purposes.

**J'ai besoin** [zhay buhswã]
d'un interprète [dũn‿ãtairpret]
d'une attestation pour mon assurance.
[doon‿atestasyõ poor mon‿asyoorõs]

It wasn't my fault.

Je ne suis pas coupable.
[zhuh nuh swee pa koopabl]

I've got nothing to do with it.

Je n'ai rien à faire avec ça.
[zhuh nay ryãn‿a fair‿avek sa]

* Quand/Où est-ce que ça c'est
passé? [kõ/oo esk sa say pasay]
* Remplissez, s'il vous plaît!
[rõpleesay seel voo play]
* Où habitez vous ici/en
Angleterre/aux États Unis?
[oo abeetay voo eesee/
õn‿õngluhtair/ohz‿aytas‿oonee]

When/Where did it happen?

Fill this in, please!

What's your address here/in England/in the
United States?

# Emergencies

▶ (See also breakdown, accident, page 24, and At the hospital, page 75)

* Attention! [atõsyõ]
* Danger (de mort)!
[dõzhay (duh mor)]
* Sortie de secours
[sortee duh suhkoor]

Help!

Caution!
(serious) Danger!

Emergency Exit

Au secours! [oh suhkoor]

# Opening times

### When does ... open/close?
the supermarket
the department store
the bank
the post office
the museum?

### A quelle heure ouvre/ferme [a kel‿uhr oovr/fairm]
le supermarché [luh soopairmarshay]
le grand magasin [luh grõ magasã]
la banque [la bõk]
le bureau de poste [luh byooroh duh post]
le musée? [luh moosay]

Are you closed at lunch time?    Vous fermez à midi? [voo fairmay a meedee]

Is there a day you are closed?    Avez-vous un jour de repos?
[avay voo ũ zhoor duh ruhpo]

# Post office

### Where can I find
a post office
a post-box?

### S'il vous plaît, où y a–t–il [seel voo play oo yateel]
le bureau de poste [luh byooroh duh post]
une boîte à lettres? [oon bwat‿a letr]

Do you sell stamps?    Vous vendez des timbres? [voo võday day tãbr]

### I'd like
10 stamps/
special issue stamps
for postcards/letters


to England/the United
States
a phonecard, please.

### Je voudrais [zhuh voodray]
dix timbres/timbres de collection
[dee tãbr/tãbr duh koleksyõ]
pour des cartes postales/lettres
[poor day kart postal/letr]

pour l'Angleterre/pour les États Unis
[poor lõngluhtair/poor lez‿aytas‿oonee]
une télécarte. [oon telaykart]

By airmail.    Par avion. [par avyõ]
Express, please.    Par exprès, s'il vous plaît. [par expray seel voo play]

* Poste restante. [post restõt]    Poste restante.

Do you have any mail for me?    Est-ce qu'il y a du courrier pour moi?
[eskeelya doo kooree-ay poor mwa]

My name is ...    Je m'appelle ... [zhuh mapel]

I would like to send a packet/    Je voudrais expédier un petit paquet/
a telegram.    un télégramme. [zhuh voodray expaydee-ay ũ
puhtee pakay/ũ telaygram]

How much do you charge for    Quel est le tarif par mot?
one word?    [kel‿ay luh tareef par mo]

I'd like to make a phone call    Je voudrais téléphoner en Angleterre/
to England/the United States.    aux États Unis. [zhuh voodray telayfonay
õn‿õngluhtair/ohz‿aytas‿oonee]

Can I call directly?    Puis-je téléphoner directement?
[pweezhuh telayfonay deerektuhmõ]

▶ (See also telecommunication, page 81)

Can I send a fax to ...from    Puis-je envoyer ici un fax à ...?
here?    [pweezh‿õvwayay eesee ũ fax a]

What do you charge for that?    Quel est le prix? [kel‿ay luh pree]

# Radio and television

**On which wavelength can I pick up**
the traffic report
English radio programmes?

What time is the news?

Do you have a TV guide?

What channels do you get?

**A quelle fréquence est-ce que je peux recevoir**
[a kel fraykōs eskuh zhuh puh ruhsuhvwar]
l'inforoute [lãforoot]
des émissions anglaises? [dayz‿emeesyō ōglez]

A quelle heure y a-t-il les informations?
[a kel‿uhr ee‿yateel layz‿ãformasyō]

Vous avez un programme de télé?
[vooz‿avay ũ program duh telay]

Quelles chaînes peut-on recevoir?
[kel shen puht‿ō ruhsuhvwar]

# Telecommunications

**(Where) can I**
make a phone call
buy a phonecard?

**Is there ... here?**
a phone box

a public phone
a payphone/cardphone

Can I send an e-mail (from here)?

Can you change this?

I need coins for the telephone.

Do you have a phonebook for ...?

Can I dial direct to ...?

A long-distance call to ..., please!

**(Où) Est-ce que je peux** [(oo) eskuh zhuh puh]
téléphoner [telayfonay]
acheter une télécarte? [ashuhtay oon telaykart]

**Y a-t-il ici** [ee‿yateel‿eesee]
une cabine téléphonique
[oon kabeen telayfoneek]
un téléphone public [ũ telayfon poobleek]
un téléphone à jetons/à cartes
[ũ telayfon‿a zhuhtō/a kart]
Puis-je envoyer un courrier électronique (d'ici)?
[pweezhuh‿ōvwyay ũ kooree-ay elektroneek]

Vous avez de la petite monnaie, s'il vous plaît?
[vooz‿avay duh la puhteet monay seel voo play]

J'ai besoin de pièces pour téléphoner.
[zhay buhswã duh pee-es poor telayfonay]

Puis-je avoir un annuaire de ...?
[pweezhuh‿avwar ũn‿anyoo-air duh]

Puis-je téléphoner directement à ...?
[pweezhuh telayfonay deerektuhmō a]

Je voudrais avoir une communication
interurbaine à ...! [zhuh voodray‿avwar‿oon
komooneekasyō ãtairuhrben a]

## Phoning in France

There are very few phone boxes left in France which accept coins. Phonecards, **télécartes** [telaykart], with 50 or 120 stored units, are sold in post offices and in tobacconists.

You will need to understand the following instructions:

**décrocher** lift the receiver – **introduire 2FF minimum** insert at least 2 francs

(one unit = three minutes) – **numéroter** dial.

Prefixes for international calls:
United Kingdom:      00 44
Republic of Ireland: 00 353
United States:       00 1

Emergency numbers (free):
Police: 17        Fire brigade: 18
Information: 19

| | |
|---|---|
| How long do I have to wait? | Il me faut attendre combien de temps?<br>[eel muh foht‿atõdr kõbyã duh tõ] |
| What's the charge per minute to …? | Combien coûte la minute pour téléphoner à …?<br>[kõbyã koot la meenoot poor telayfonay a] |
| Is there a cheap rate at night time? | Y a-t-il un tarif de nuit?<br>[ee‿yateel ũ tareef duh nwee] |
| I'd like to make a reversed charge call. | Je voudrais téléphoner en P. C. V.<br>[zhuh voodray telayfonay õ paysayvay] |

| | |
|---|---|
| * Occupé. [okoopay] | Engaged. |
| * Ça ne répond pas.<br>[sa nuh raypõ pa] | There's no reply. |

| | |
|---|---|
| Hello! | Allô! [alo] |
| Who's calling? | Qui est à l'appareil? [kee‿ayt‿a laparay] |
| This is … | C'est … à l'appareil. [say … a laparay] |
| Can I speak to Mr/Mrs … ? | Je voudrais parler à Monsieur/Madame …<br>[zhuh voodray parlay a muhsyuh/madam] |

| | |
|---|---|
| * A l'appareil. [a laparay] | Speaking. |
| * Je regrette, il/elle n'est pas là.<br>[zhuh ruhgret eel/el nay pa la] | Sorry, he/she is not here at the moment. |

| | |
|---|---|
| Do you speak English? | Parlez-vous anglais?<br>[parlay vooz‿õglay] |
| When is he/she back? | Quand sera-t-il/sera-t-elle de retour?<br>[kõ suhratteel/suhratel duh ruhtoor] |
| I'll call again later. | Je rappellerai plus tard. [zhuh rapeluhray ploo tar] |
| Please tell him/her that I called. | Veuillez lui dire que j'ai appelé.<br>[vuhyay lwee deer kuh zhay apuhlay] |
| My number is … | Mon numéro est le … [mõ noomairo ay luh] |
| Thank you, goodbye! | Merci, au revoir! [mairsee oh ruhvwar] |

## Toilets

| | |
|---|---|
| Where are the toilets please? | Où sont les toilettes, s'il vous plaît?<br>[oo sõ lay twalet seel voo play] |
| Is there a public toilet around here? | Y a-t-il des toilettes publiques ici?<br>[ee‿yateel day twalet poobleek‿eesee] |

| | |
|---|---|
| * Dames./Messieurs.<br>[dam/muhsyuh] | Ladies./Gentlemen. |

## Tipping

| | |
|---|---|
| Is service included? | Le service est compris?<br>[luh sairvees‿ay kõpree] |
| How much does one tip? | On donne combien de pourboire?<br>[õ don kõbyã duh poorbwar] |
| That's for you! | Voilà pour vous! [vwala poor voo] |
| Keep the change! | Gardez-le! [garday luh] |
| That's fine! | C'est bon! [say bõ] |

# English–French A–Z

## A

**accident** l'accident [lakseedõ] 24
**accidentally** par erreur [par_eruhr]
**accommodation** le logement
[luh lozhmõ] 32
**admission ticket** le billet d'entrée
[luh beeyay dõtray] 57
**admission** l'entrée [lõtray] 49, 57
**adult** l'adulte (m, f) [ladoolt] 28, 52
**age** l'âge [lazh] 14
**agreed** d'accord [dakor]
**air-conditioning** l'air conditionné
[lair kõdeesyõnay] 38
**air** l'air [lair]
**aircraft** l'avion [lavyõ] 29
**airport** l'aéroport [layropor] 22, 29
**alarm clock** le réveil [luh rayvay] 66
**all** tous (toutes) [toos (toot)]
**alone** seul,-e [suhl]
**ambulance** l'ambulance
[lõbyoolõs] 24, 72
**American** américain, -e [amayreekã,
amayreeken] 13, 80
**angry** furieux (furieuse)
[fyooreeyuh (fyooreeyuhz)]
**animal** l'animal [laneemal] 36
**answer machine** le répondeur
automatique
[luh raypõduhr_ohtomateek] 81
**antiques** les antiquités
[layz_õteekeetay] 69
**apartment** l'appartement
[lapartuhmõ] 32, 36
**appointment** le rendez-vous
[luh rõdayvoo] 14
**approximately** environ [õveerõ]
**arm** le bras [luh bra] 74
**Australia** l'Australie [lohstralee] 13
**Australian** australien, -ne
[ohstraleeyã, ohstraleeyen] 13
**autumn** l'automne [lohton] 19
**avenue** l'allée [lalay] 22

## B

**baby** le bébé [luh bebay]
**baby's bottle** le biberon
[luh beebuhrõ] 62, 71

**bad** mauvais,-e [mohvay,-z]
**bakery** la boulangerie [la
boolõzhuhree] 61, 64
**bank** la banque [la bõk] 77
**bar** le bistro [luh beestro] 40
**bathroom** la salle de bains
[la sal duh bã] 32
**bay** la baie [la bay] 55
**beach** la plage [la plazh] 34, 53
**beautiful** beau (belle) [boh (bel)]
**bed** le lit [luh lee] 32
**bedcovers** la couverture
[la koovairchoor]
**bedroom** la chambre [la shõbr] 32, 34
**beer** la bière [la bee-air] 48
**beginning** le début [luh daybyoo] 57
**belt** la ceinture [la sãchoor] 67
**bicycle** la bicyclette
[la beeseeklet] 22, 25, 79
**big** grand,-e [grõ,-d]
**birthday** l'anniversaire
[laneevairsair] 14
**black** noir,-e [nwar] 20
**blame** la culpabilité
[la koolpabeeleetay] 24, 78
**blood** le sang [luh sõ] 74
**blood alcohol level** le taux
d'alcoolémie [luh toh dalkoolaymee]
**blouse** le chemisier
[luh shuhmeezee-ay] 65, 67
**board, full** la pension complète
[la põsyõ kõplet] 33
**boat** le bateau [luh batoh] 29
**body** le corps [luh kor] 74
**body lotion** le lait de toilette
[lay duh twalet] 71
**book** le livre [luh leevr] 64
**bookshop** la librairie [la leebrairee] 64
**boot** la botte [la bot] 67
**border** la frontière [la frõtee-air] 21
**boring** ennuyeux (ennuyeuse)
[õnwee-uh (õnwee-uhz)]
**boss** le patron [luh patrõ] 32, 40
**bottle** la bouteille [la bootay] 42, 64
**bottle opener** l'ouvre-bouteille
[loovr bootay] 61
**bowl** le saladier [luh saladee-ay]

boy le garçon [luh garsõ] 13
bra le soutien-gorge
  [luh sootyã gorzh] 67
breakfast le petit déjeuner
  [luh puhtee dayzhuhnay] 33, 40, 44
bridge le pont [luh põ] 50, 75
bright clair,-e [klair] 20
broken cassé,-e [kasay]
broken endommagé,-e [õdomazhay]
brother le frère [luh frair] 13
brother-in-law le beau-frère
  [luh boh frair] 13
bureau de change le bureau de
  change/le change [luh byooroh duh
  shõzh/luh shõzh] 77
bus le bus [luh boos] 27, 30
bus-stop l'arrêt d'autobus
  [laray dohtoboos] 22, 27, 30
butcher la boucherie [la booshuhree] 61
button le bouton [luh bootõ]
buy acheter [ashuhtay] 58

C
cabin (on a boat) la cabine
  [la kabeen] 30
cabin (on a camp-site) la cabane
  [la kaban] 36
café le café [luh kafay] 40
called, to be s'appeler [sapuhlay]
camera l'appareil photo
  [laparay foto] 67
camera film la pellicule
  [la peleekool] 67, 69
cap le bonnet [luh bonay] 67
car park le parking
  [luh parkeeng] 23, 34, 38
car la voiture [la vwachoor] 22, 25, 79
caravan la caravane
  [la karavan] 36, 39
castle le château [luh shatoh] 50, 51
cat le chat [luh sha] 36
cathedral la cathédrale
  [la kataydral] 50
cause la cause [la cohz]
ceiling le plafond [luh plafõ] 35, 38
centimetre le centimètre
  [luh sõteemetr] 20
centre le centre [luh sõtr] 22
certificate l'attestation
  [latestasyõ] 24, 76
chain la chaîne [la shen] 25
chair la chaise [la shez]
change (money) changer [shõzhay]

chapel la chapelle [la shapel] 50
charter flight le vol charter
  [luh vol chartair] 29
cheap bon marché [bõ marshay]
chemist la pharmacie [la farmasee] 76;
  la droguerie [la drogree] 70
cheque le chèque [luh shek] 34, 77
child l'enfant (m, f) [lõfõ] 13
church l'église [laygleez] 50
cigarette la cigarette [la seegaret] 71
cinema le cinéma
  [luh seenayma] 57
circular tour le voyage circulaire
  [luh vwayazh seerkyoolair]
clean propre [propr]
cleaning (dry) le nettoyage (à sec)
  [luh netwayazh (a sek)] 66
clear clair,-e [klair]
clever intelligent,-e [ãteleezhõ,-t]
closed fermé,-e [fairmay] 80
clothing les vêtements [lay vetmõ] 65
coach le car [luh kar] 52
coast la côte [la koht] 53
coat le manteau [luh mõtoh] 67
code, dialling l'indicatif
  [lãdeekateef] 81
coin la pièce de monnaie
  [la pee-es duh monay] 39
cold froid,-e [frwã,-d] 19, 43
colour la couleur [la kooluhr] 20
comb le peigne [luh penyuh] 71
company l'entreprise [lõtruhpreez]
compartment le compartiment
  [luh kõparteemõ] 27
complaint la réclamation
  [la rayklamasyõ] 35, 42
concert le concert [luh kõsair] 57
condom le préservatif
  [luh prayzairvateef] 71
confusion la confusion [la kõfyoozyõ]
contraceptive le contraceptif
  [luh kõtrasepteef] 71, 76
contract le contrat [luh kõtra] 22
cooked cuit,-e [kwee,-t]
corkscrew le tire-bouchon
  [luh teer booshõ] 61
correct juste [zhoost]
cosmetics les articles de toilette
  [layz˗arteekl duh twalet] 71
costs les frais [lay fray]
cotton wool le coton
  [luh kotõ] 71
cotton le coton [luh kotõ] 66

cottonwool buds les cotons tiges
[lay kotõ teezh] 71
couchette la couchette [la cooshet] 28
country estate la propriété rurale
[la propree-aytay rooral] 22, 32
country road la chaussée
[la shohsay] 22
country le pays [luh payee]
countryside le paysage
[luh payzazh] 51
cousin le cousin, -e
[luh koozã, -een] 13
crafts l'artisanat d'art
[larteezana dar] 69
credit card la carte de crédit
[la kart duh kredee] 34, 77
cruise la croisière [la krwazee-air] 29
cry (vb) pleurer [pluhray]
cup la tasse [la tas] 43
currency la monnaie [la monay] 77
current le courant [luh koorõ] 37, 39
customs la douane [la dwan] 21
cutlery le couvert [luh koovair] 43
cycling, to go faire du vélo
[fair doo vayloh]

**D**
damp humide [oomeed]
dance (vb) danser [dõsay] 58, 59
danger le danger [luh dõnzhay] 54
daughter la fille [la fee] 13
day le jour [luh zhoor] 12, 19
day-ticket la carte journalière
[la kart zhoornalee-air] 30, 49
dear cher (chère) [shair (shair)]
deep profond,-e [profõ,-d]
degree le degré [luh duhgray] 19, 73
dentist le dentiste [luh dõteest] 74
department store le grand magasin
[luh grõ maguhzã] 61
departure le départ
[luh daypar] 27, 30
desert le dessert [luh desair] 41, 47
detergent le détergent
[luh daytairzhõ] 71
die mourir [mooreer]
diesel le gasole [luh gazol] 24
difference la différence [la deefayrõs]
different différent,-e [deefayrõ,-t]
difficult difficile [deefeeseel]
direct flight le vol sans escale
[luh vol sõs_eskal] 29
direct direct,-e [deerekt]

direction la direction
[la deereksyõ] 22, 30
dirty sale [sal]
discount la réduction [la raydooksyõ]
district le quartier [luh kartyay] 22
disturb déranger [dayrõzhay]
diversion la déviation
[la dayvee-asyõ] 23
dizzy pris,-e de vertiges
[pree,-z duh vairteezh]
doctor le médecin [luh maydsã] 24, 72
dog le chien [luh shyã] 36
donkey l'âne [lan]
door la porte [la port]
doubt la doute [la doot]
dress la robe [la rob] 65
drink (vb) boire [bwar] 48
drink la boisson [la bwasõ] 48
drinking water l'eau potable
[loh potabl] 28, 39
driving licence le permis de conduire
[luh permee duh kõdweer] 21
drunk ivre [eevr]
dummy la sucette [la sooset] 71

**E**
early tôt [toh]
ear-rings les boucles d'oreille [lay
bookl doray] 67
earth la terre [la tair]
east l'est [lest] 22
edible mangeable [mõzhabl]
education l'éducation [laydookasyõ]
embassy l'ambassade [lõbasad] 21
emergency alarm le frein d'alarme
[luh frã dalarm] 27, 30
emergency telephone la borne de
détresse [la born duh daytres] 24, 79
empty vide [veed]
engine le moteur [luh motuhr] 25, 27
England l'Angleterre [lõgluhtair] 13, 80
English anglais, -e [õglay, -z] 13, 80
Enter! Entrez! [õtray]
entertainment l'amusement
[lamoozmõ] 57
entrance l'entrée [lõtray] 22, 57
environment l'environnement
[lõveeronuhmõ] 56
environmental protection la
conservation de la nature
[la põsairvasyõ duh la nachoor] 56
estate agent l'agent immobilier
[lazhõ imobeelee-ay]

**evening meal** le dîner
[luh deenay] 16, 40
**evening** le soir [luh swar] 12, 18
**events calender** le programme des
spectacles
[luh program day spektakl] 49
**everything** tout [too]
**excursion** l'excursion [lexkoorsyõ] 52
**exhausted** épuisé,-e [aypweezay]
**exit** la sortie [la sortee] 27, 57
**expensive** cher (chère) [shair (shair)]

**F**

**factory** l'usine [loozeen]
**faithful** fidèle [feedel]
**family** la famille [la famee] 13
**far** loin [lwa]
**farewell** les adieux [layz‿adyuh] 12
**fashion** la mode [la mod] 65
**fast** vite [veet]
**fat** gros (grosse) [gro (gros)]
**father** le père [luh pair] 13
**fax** le fax [luh fax] 35, 80
**fear** la peur [la puhr] 72, 78
**ferry** le ferry [luh feree] 29
**field** le champ [luh shõ] 56
**film** le film [luh feelm] 67, 69
**fine** *(police)* l'amende [lamõd] 78
**finger** le doigt [luh dwa] 74
**fire** le feu [luh fuh] 79
**fire brigade** les pompiers
[lay põpee-ay] 24
**fire extinguisher** l'extincteur
[lextãktuhr] 24, 79
**fish shop** la poissonnerie
[la pwasonuhree] 45, 64
**flash** le flash [luh flash] 67
**flat** l'appartement [lapartuhmõ] 32, 36
**flavour** le goût [luh goo] 40
**flea market** le marché aux puces
[luh marshay oh poos] 61
**flight** *(scheduled)* le vol de ligne [luh
vol duh leenye] 29
**flight attendant**
le steward [luh stoo-ar],
l'hôtesse de l'air [lohtes duh lair] 29
**flight** le vol [luh vol] 29
**flirt** flirter [fluhrtay]
**flowers** les fleurs [lay fluhr] 61
**fly** la mouche [la moosh]
**food** les alimentations
[layz‿aleemõtasyõ] 62, 64
**football** le football [luh footbol] 54

**forbidden** interdit,-e [ãtairdee,-t]
**foreigner** l'étranger (l'étrangère)
[laytrõzhay (laytrõzhair)] 13
**forest, primeval** la forêt vierge
[la foray vee-airzh] 56
**forget** oublier [ooblee-ay]
**fork** la fourchette [la foorshet] 43
**fragile** fragil,-e [frazheel]
**France** la France [la frõs] 13, 80
**free** gratuit [gratwee]; libre [leebr]
**French** français,-e [frõsay,-z] 13
**fresh** frais (fraîche) [fray (fresh)]
**Friday** vendredi [võdruhdee] 19
**friend** l'ami(e) *(m, f)* [lamee] 14
**fruit** les fruits [lay frwee] 62
**full up** rassasié,-e [rasasee-ay]
**full** plein (pleine) [plã (plen)]
**fuse** le fusible [luh foozeebl] 25

**G**

**garden** le jardin [luh zhardã] 50
**gentlemen** les messieurs
[lay mesyuh] 83
**genuine** véritable [vayreetabl]
**girl** la fille [la fee] 13
**glass** le verre [luh vair] 42, 43
**glasses** les lunettes [lay loonet] 70
**gloves** les gants [lay gõ] 67
**goal** le but [luh boot] 22, 54
**gone away** parti,-e [partee]
**good** bon (bonne) [bõ (bon)]
**government** le gouvernement [luh
goovairnuhmõ]
**granddaughter** la petite fille
[la puhteet fee] 13
**grandfather** le grand-père
[luh grõpair] 13
**grandmother** la grand-mère
[la grõmair] 13
**grandson** le petit fils
[luh puhtee fees] 13
**greet** saluer [saloo-ay]
**ground-floor** le rez-de-chaussée
[luh ray duh shohsay] 32
**group** le groupe [luh groop] 49
**guarantee** la garantie [la garõtee]
**guest-house** la pension
[la põsyõ] 32, 39

**H**

**hair** les cheveux [lay shuhvuh] 70
**hairbrush** la brosse à cheveux
[la bros‿a shuhvuh] 71

**hairdresser** le coiffeur [luh kwafuhr]
**hairspray** la laque [la lak] 71
**hand-bag** le sac à main
  [luh sak (a mã] 61, 78
**hand-luggage** les bagages à main [lay
  bagazh_a mã] 29
**happy** heureux (heureuse)
  [uhruh (uhruhz)]
**harbour** le port [luh por] 22, 29, 50
**hard** dur,-e [joor]
**hat** le chapeau [luh shapoh] 67
**head** la tête [la tet] 74
**healthy** en bonne santé [õ bõ sõtay]
**heating** le chauffage
  [luh shofazh] 35, 38
**heavy** lourd,-e [loor,-d]
**help** *(vb)* aider [ayday]
**Help!** Au secours! [oh suhkoor] 79
**high** haut,-e [oh,-t]
**hobbies** les loisirs [lay lwazeer] 53
**holiday villa** la maison de vacances
  [la mayzõ duh vakõs] 36
**holiday** le jour férié
  [luh zhoor fayree-ay] 77
**holidays** les vacances [lay vakõs] 36
**home country** le pays natal
  [luh payee natal] 13
**home** à la maison [a la mayzõ]
**home-made** fait maison [fay mayzõ]
**hospital** l'hôpital [lopeetal] 75
**hot** chaud,-e [shoh,-d]
**hour** l'heure [luhr] 19
**house** la maison [la mayzõ] 36
**hunger** la faim [la fã] 40
**husband** le mari [luh maree] 13
**hydrofoil** l'hydroglisseur
  [leedrogleesuhr] 29

**I**

**ill** malade [malad] 72
**important** important,-e [ãportõ,-t]
**impossible** impossible [ãposeebl]
**information** le renseignement
  [luh rõsenyuhmõ] 28, 49
**inhabitant** l'habitant [labeetõ]
**injured** blessé,-e [blesay]
**innocent** innocent,-e [eenosõ,-t]
**insurance** l'assurance [lasyoorõs] 22
**intelligent** intelligent,-e [ãteleezhõ,-t]
**interesting** intéressant,-e [ãtayresõ,-t]
**invalid** *(pass)* périmé [payreemay] 21
**investigation** l'examen
  [lãnvesteegasyõ]

**Ireland** l'Irlande [leerlõd]
**Irish** irlandais, -e [eerlõday, -z]
**island** l'île [leel] 50

**J**

**jacket** la veste [la vest] 65
**jeans** le jean [le zheen] 65
**jellyfish** la méduse [la maydooz] 53, 72
**jeweller** le bijoutier
  [luh beezhootee-ay] 66
**jewellery** les bijoux [lay beezhoo] 66
**joke** la plaisanterie [la playzõtuhree]
**journey** le voyage [luh vwayazh] 21
**judgement** le jugement [luh zhoozhmõ]
**jumper** le pullover [luh poolovair] 65
**junk shop** la brocante [la brokõt]

**K**

**key** la clé [la klay] 36, 39
**kilo** le kilo [luh keelo] 20, 64
**kiosk** le kiosque [luh kee-osk] 61
**kiss** le baiser [luh bayzay]
**knife** le couteau [luh kootoh] 43
**knitwear** les tricotages
  [lay treekotazh] 67

**L**

**ladies** les dames [lay dam] 83
**lake** le lac [luh lak] 53, 56
**language** la langue [la lõg] 13, 15
**large** grand,-e [grõ,-d]
**late** tard [tar] 19
**laundry** la blanchisserie
  [la blõsheesuhree] 66
**lawn** le gazon [luh gazõ]
**leather** le cuir [luh kweer] 69
**leather goods** la maroquinerie
  [la marokeenuhree] 69
**left** à gauche [a gohsh]
**left luggage locker** la consigne
  automatique
  [la kõseeny_ohtomateek] 28
**left luggage office** la consigne
  [la kõseenyuh] 28
**leg** la jambe [la zhõb] 73
**letter** la lettre [la letr] 64, 80
**letter box** la boîte aux lettres
  [la bwat_oh letr] 80
**life jacket** le gilet de sauvetage
  [luh geelay duh sohvuhtazh] 53, 55
**lifeboat** le canot de sauvetage
  [luh kano duh sohvuhtaj] 29, 53
**lift** l'ascenseur [lasõsuhr] 38

light *(electric)* la lumière
  [la loomee-air] 35, 38
light léger (légère) [layzhay (layzhair)]
lightning l'éclair [layklair] 19
linen le lin [luh lã] 66
lipstick le rouge à lèvres
  [luh roozh_a levr] 71
litre le litre [luh leetr] 64
little peu [puh]
live *(vb)* vivre [veevr]
live in habiter [abeetay]
local train le train suburbain
  [luh trã suhboorbã] 27
long long (longue) [lõ (lõg)]
lorry le camion [luh kamee-õ] 23
lost property office le bureau des
  objets trouvés [luh byooroh
  dayz_obzhay troovay] 49, 78
lot, a beaucoup (de) [bohkoo (duh)]
lounger la chaise longue
  [la shez lõg] 53
love *(vb)* aimer [aymay]
luggage les bagages [lay bagazh] 28, 38
lunch le déjeuner
  [luh dayzhuhnay] 16, 40

**M**
magazine la revue [la ruhvoo] 64
make-up le maquillage [makeeyazh] 71
man l'homme [lom]
manager le directeur
  [luh deerektuhr] 32
many beaucoup (de) [bohkoo (duh)]
map la carte géographique
  [la kart zhayografeek] 49
market (hall) le marché (couvert) [luh
  marshay (koovair)] 51, 61
marriage le mariage [luh maree-azh]
married couple le couple marié
  [luh koopl maree-ay] 13
married marié,-e [maree-ay] 14
matches les allumettes
  [layz_aloomet] 71
material le tissu [luh teesoo] 66
mattress (inflatable) le matelas
  (pneumatique) [luh matla
  (noomateek)] 53
meal le repas [luh ruhpa] 40
medication le médicament [luh
  maydeekamõ] 73
memory le souvenir [luh soovuhneer]
menu la carte [la kart] 41, 44
metre le mètre [luh metr] 20

midday le midi [luh meedee] 18
misfortune le malheur [luh maluhr] 79
Miss Madamoiselle [madmwazel] 12
mistake l'erreur [leruhr] 27, 78
modern moderne [modairn]
moment l'instant [lãstõ] 14
monastery le monastère
  [luh monastair] 50
Monday lundi [lũdee] 19
money l'argent [larzhõ] 77
month le mois [luh mwa] 19
morning le matin [luh matã] 12, 18
mosquito repellent la crème
  antimoustique
  [la krem õteemoosteek] 71
mosquito la moustique [la moosteek]
mother la mère [la mair] 13
motor home le camping-car
  [luh kõpeeng kar] 22, 37
motorway l'autoroute
  [lohtoroot] 22, 23
motorway toll le péage
  [luh payazh] 22
motor-cycle la moto [la moto] 22, 25
mountain la montagne
  [la mõtãnyuh] 50, 56
mouthwash le gargarisme
  [luh gargareezm] 71
Mr Monsieur [muhsyuhr] 12
Mrs Madame [madam] 12
music la musique [la moozeek] 57, 58

**N**
nail file la lime à ongles
  [la leem_a ãgl] 71
nail scissors les ciseaux à ongles
  [lay seezoh a õgl] 71
nail varnish le vernis à ongles
  [luh vairnees_a ãgl] 71
nail-varnish remover le dissolvant
  [luh deesolvõ] 71
naked nu,-e [noo]
name le nom [luh nõ] 12
napkin la serviette [la servee-et] 43
nappies les langes [le lõzh] 71
natural fibre la fibre naturelle
  [la feebr nachoorel] 66
nature la nature [la nachoor] 56
naughty méchant,-e [mayshõ,-t]
nausea la nausée [la nohzay] 72
necessary nécessaire [nesesair]
neighbour le voisin [luh vwazã] 13
nephew le neveu [luh nuhvuh] 13

New Zealand *(adj)* néo-zélandais,-e [nayozaylõday, -z]
New Zealand la Nouvelle Zélande [la noovel zaylõd]
new nouveau (nouvelle) [noovoh (noovel)]; (brand new) neuf (neuve) [nuhf (nuhv)]
news les informations [layz˷âformasyõ] 81
newspaper le journal [luh zhoornal] 64
nice gentil,-le [zhõtee,-y]
niece la nièce [la nee-es] 13
night la nuit [la nwee] 12, 18
no non [nõ]
noise le bruit [luh brwee]
noisy bruyant,-e [brweeyã, -t]
non-smokers non-fumeurs [nõ foomuhr] 28
normal normal,-e [normal]
north le nord [luh nor] 22
number le chiffre [luh sheefr]
number le numéro [luh noomairo] 22, 81

**O**

occupied occupé,-e [okoopay]
office l'office [lofees] 80
old vieux (vieille) [vyuh (veeyay)]
open ouvert,-e [oovair,-t] 80
opening times les heures d'ouverture [layz˷uhr doovairchoor] 80
optician l'opticien [lopteesyã] 70
other l'autre [lohtr]
owner le propriétaire [luh propree-aytair]

**P**

package le petit paquet [luh puhtee pakay] 80
pain les douleurs [lay dooluhr] 72, 73
pair la paire [la pair] 20
palace le palais [luh palay] 50
parasol le parasol [luh parasol] 53
parents les parents [lay parõ] 13
part la partie [la partee]
party la fête [la fet] 60, 77
passage le passage [luh pasazh] 22
passenger le passager [luh pasazhay]
passport le passeport [luh paspor] 21, 78
past *(noun)* le passé [luh pasay]
path le chemin [luh shuhmã] 22
pay *(vb)* payer [payay] 34, 43, 64

pedestrian le piéton [luh pee-aytõ] 22
pension la pension [la põsyõ] 32, 39
people le peuple [luh puhpl]
percent pour cent [poor sõ]
performance le spectacle [luh spektakl]
perfume le parfum [luh parfü] 71
petrol station la station-service [la stasyõ sairvees] 24
petrol l'essence [lesõs] 23, 24
pH-neutral pH neutre [pay ash nootr]
photograph la photo [la foto] 67, 69
picture l'image [leemazh] 50
pillow l'oreiller [lorayay] 35, 38
Pity! Dommage! [domazh] 14
place of interest la curiosité [la kyooree-oseetay]
place l'endroit [lãdrwa] 22
plain la plaine [la plen] 56
plant la plante [la plõt] 56, 61
plate l'assiette [lasyet] 43
platform le quai [luh kay] 27, 28
play *(vb)* jouer [zhoo-ay]
poisonous toxique [toxeek]
police officer l'agent de police [lazhõ duh polees] 78
police la police [la polees] 24, 78
politics la politique [la poleeteek]
poor pauvre [pohvr]
port le port [luh por] 22, 29, 50
possible possible [poseebl]
post office le bureau de poste [luh byooroh duh post] 77, 80
post le courrier [luh kooree-ay] 80
postcode le code postal [luh kod postal]
pottery la céramique [la sayrameek] 69
powder la poudre [la poodr] 71
pregnant enceinte [õsãt] 73
prescription l'ordonnance [lordonõs] 76
present le cadeau [luh kadoh] 69
pretty joli,-e [zholee]
price le prix [luh pree] 61
priest le prêtre [luh pretr]
profession la profession [la profesyõ] 14
programme le programme [luh program] 81
proprietor le patron [luh patrõ] 40
pullover le pullover [luh poolovair] 65
punctual à l'heure [a luhr]
pyjamas le pyjama [luh peezhama] 67

**Q**

quality la qualité [la kaleetay] 61
question la question [la kestyõ] 16
quick vite [veet]
quiet tranquille [trõkeel]

**R**

radio la radio [la radyo] 67, 81
rain la pluie [la ploo-ee] 19
raincoat l'imperméable
  [lãpairmayabl] 65
rape le viol [luh vee-ol] 79
rare rare [rahr]
razor-blade les lames de rasoir
  [lay lam duh raswah] 71
ready prêt,-e [pray, pret]
reason la raison [la rayzõ]
receipt la quittance [la keetõs] 43, 76
reception la réception
  [la raysepsyõ] 32
recommend recommander
  [ruhkomõday]
records les disques [lay deesk] 61
refuse les ordures [layz ordjoor] 39
relationship la liaison
  [la lee-aysõ] 27, 30
relative le parent [luh parõ] 13
residence le domicile
  [luh domeeseel] 79
responsible compétent,-e [kõpaytõ,-t]
restaurant le restaurant
  [luh restohrõ] 40, 42
result le résultat [luh raysoolta] 54
rich riche [reesh]
right, on the à droite [a drwat]
river le fleuve [luh fluhv] 56
riverbank le bord [luh bor] 53
roadside restaurant le relais routier
  [luh ruhlay rootee-ay] 40
room la salle [la sal] 51
round rond,-e [rõ,-d]
rubber boot la botte en caoutchouc
  [la bot õ ka-oochoo] 67
rucksack le sac à dos
  [luh sak a doh] 56

**S**

sad triste [treest]
safe sûr,-e [syoor]
safety belt la ceinture de sécurité [la
  sãtoor duh saykooreetay] 25
safety la sécurité
  [la saykooreetay] 54, 79

sale la vente [la võt] 61; les soldes
  [lay sold] 61
sandals les sandales [lay sõdal] 67
sanitary towels les serviettes
  hygiéniques
  [lay sairvee-et eezheneek] 71
satisfied content,-e [kõtõ,-t]
Saturday samedi [samdee] 19
saucepan le pot [luh po] 38
scarf le foulard [luh foolar] 67;
  l'écharpe [laysharp] 67
scissors les ciseaux [lay seezoh] 71
Scotland l'Écosse [laykos]
Scottish écossais, -e [aykosay, -z]
sea (rough) la mer (démontée)
  [la mair daymõtay] 29, 53
sea urchin l'oursin [loorsã] 53, 72
sea la mer [la mair] 53
seasickness le mal de mer
  [luh mal duh mair] 29, 72
season la saison [la sayzõ] 19
seat le siège [luh see-ezh] 27, 30
second la seconde [la suhkõd] 18
self-service le libre service
  [luh leebr sairvees] 40, 61
send envoyer [õvwayay]
sex le sex [luh sex]
shirt la chemise [la shuhmeez] 65
shoe la chaussure [la shohsyoor] 65
shoe cream le cirage [luh seerazh] 65
shop la boutique [la booteek] 65;
  le magasin [luh magazã] 61
shop window la vitrine
  [la veetreen] 61
shopping centre le centre commercial
  [luh sõtr komersyal] 61
shopping, to go faire des courses
  [fair day koors] 61
shore le bord [luh bor] 53
short court,-e [koor,-t]
shorts le short [luh short] 67
shower la douche [la doosh] 33, 38
sign le panneau [luh panoh] 23, 28, 54
signature la signature
  [la seenyachoor] 78
signpost le poteau indicateur
  [luh potoh ãdeekatuhr] 22
silence le silence [luh seelõs]
silk la soie [la swa] 66
single célibataire [sayleebatair]
sister la soeur [la suhr] 13
sister-in-law la belle-soeur
  [la bel suhr] 13

situation la situation [la seechoo-asyō]
skirt la jupe [la zhoop] 65
sky le ciel [luh see-el] 19
sleeper car le wagon-lit
  [luh vagō lee] 28
sleeve la manche [la mōsh] 65
slim mince [mãs]
slow lent,-e [lõ,-t]
small petit,-e [puhtee,-t]
smell l'odeur [loduhr] 40
snack la casse-croûte [la kas kroot] 40
soap (liquid) le savon liquide
  [luh savō leekeed] 71
soap le savon [luh savō] 71
socks les chaussettes [lay shohset] 65
soft souple [soopl]
solicitor l'avocat [lavoka] 79
some quelques [kelk]
someone quelqu'un [kelk‿ũ]
son le fils [luh fees] 13
sorry pardon [pardō] 14
south le sud [luh sood] 22
souvenir le souvenir [luh soovuhneer]
special offer l'offre spéciale
  [lofr spaysyal] 61
special rate le tarif spécial
  [luh tareef spaysee-al] 29
specialities les spécialités
  [lay spaysee-aleetay] 41
spectacles les lunettes [lay loonet] 70
speed la vitesse [la veetes] 22, 27
spoilt pourri,-e [pooree]
sponge l'éponge [laypōzh] 71
spoon la cuillère [la kweeyair] 43
sport le sport [luh spor] 54
sports articles les articles de sport
  [layz‿arteekl duh spor] 61
spring la source [la soors] 50
spring (time of year) le printemps
  [luh prãtō] 19
square la place [la plas] 22, 28
stadium le stade [luh stad] 39, 54
staircase l'escalier [leskiyay]
stamp le timbre [luh tãbr] 80
stand-by stand by [stōd by] 29
starter (cold) le hors d'oeuvre
  [luh orduhvr]; (warm) l'entrée
  [lōtray] 41, 44
state l'état [layta]
station la gare [la gar] 22, 27
stationery les articles de papeterie
  [layz‿arteekl duh papetuhree] 64
stiff raide [red]

stone la pierre [la pee-air]
stopover l'escale [leskal]
storey l'étage [laytazh] 32
storm l'orage [lorazh] 19
straight on tout droit [too drwa]
street la rue [la roo] 22
studio l'atelier [latelee-ay] 24
stupid stupide [stoopeed]
suburb la banlieue [la bōlyuh] 22
suede le daim [luh dã] 69
suit le costume [luh kostoom] 67
suit (lady's) le tailleur [luh tiyuhr] 67
suitcase la valise [la valees] 28, 29
summer l'été [laytay] 19
sun le soleil [luhl solay] 19
Sunday dimanche [deemōsh] 19
sunglasses les lunettes de soleil
  [lay loonet duh solay] 70
suntan lotion la crème solaire
  [la krem solar] 55, 70
supermarket le supermarché
  [luh soopairmarshay] 61
supplement le supplément
  [luh sooplaymō] 27, 30
surprise la surprise [la suhrpreez]
sweatshirt le sweatshirt
  [le swetshert] 67
sweets la confiserie [la kōfeesuhree] 61;
  les bonbons [lay bōbō]
swimming pool la piscine
  [la peeseen] 34, 53
synthetic synthétique [sãteteek]

T

table la table [la tabl] 40
tablets les comprimés
  [lay kōpreemay] 73
take off (aeroplane) le décollage
  [luh daykolazh] 29
tampons les tampons hygiéniques
  [lay tōpō eezheneek] 71
taxi le taxi [luh taxee] 31
telegram le télégramme
  [luh telaygram] 80
telephone call la communication
  [la komooneekasyō] 81
telephone directory l'annuaire
  téléphonique
  [lanoo-air telayfoneek] 81
telephone le téléphone
  [luh telayfon] 81, 83
temperature la température
  [la tōpayrachoor] 19

**terminus** le terminus
[luh termeenoos] 27, 30
**terrible** affreux (affreuse)
[afruh, afruhz]
**thank you** merci [mairsee] 14
**theatre** le théâtre [luh tayatr] 51
**theft** le vol [luh vol] 79
**thin** mince [mãs]
**thing** la chose [la shoz]
**thirst** la soif [la swaf] 40
**this** ce/cette [suh/set]
**Thursday** jeudi [zhuhdee] 19
**ticket inspector** le contrôleur
[luh kõtroluhr] 27, 30
**ticket office** le guichet
[luh geeshay] 27, 30
**ticket** le ticket [luh teekay] 27, 30, 57
**tie** la cravate [la kravat] 67
**tights** le collant [luh kolõ] 67
**time** le temps [luh tõ] 18
**timetable** l'horaire [lorair] 27, 30
**timid** timide [teemeed]
**tip** le pourboire [luh poorbwah] 83
**tired** fatigué,-e [fateegay]
**tiring** fatigant,-e [fateegõ,-t]
**tobacco** le tabac [luh taba] 71
**tobacconist** le tabac [luh taba] 71
**toilet** les toilettes
[lay twalet] 28, 32, 83
**toilet paper** le papier hygiénique
[luh papee-ay eezheneek] 35, 71, 83
**too much** trop [tro]
**toothbrush** la brosse à dents
[la bros‿a dõ] 71
**toothpaste** le dentifrice
[luh dõteefrees] 71
**total** la somme [la som]
**tourist office** l'office de tourisme
[lofees duh tooreezm] 49
**tourist** le touriste [luh tooreest] 49
**tow away** dépanner [daypanay] 24
**towel** la serviette de toilette
[la sairvee-et duh twalet] 35, 38
**tower** la tour [la toor] 51
**town centre** le centre ville
[luh sõtr veel] 22, 50
**town hall** la mairie [la mairee]; (in
large towns) l'hôtel de ville [lohtel
duh veel] 50
**town map** le plan de ville
[luh plõ duh veel] 49
**town** la ville [la veel] 22, 51
**toys** les jouets [lay zhoo-ay] 61

**traffic lights** les feux [lay fuh] 22
**traffic** la circulation
[la seerkoolasyõ] 23
**train** le train [luh trã] 27
**trainers** les baskets [lay basket] 65
**tram** le tram [luh tram] 30
**translator** l'interprète *(m, f)*
[lãterpret] 79
**travel agency** l'agence de voyage
[lazhõs duh vwayazh] 49
**travel guide** le guide touristique
[luh geed tooreesteek] 52
**travellers' cheque** le chèque de
voyage [luh shek duh vwayazh] 34, 77
**tree** l'arbre [larbr] 56
**trousers** le pantalon [luh põtalõ] 65
**truck** le camion [luh kameeyõ] 23
**true** vrai,-e [vray]
**T-shirt** le T-shirt [luh tee shirt] 65
**Tuesday** mardi [mardee] 19
**tunnel** le tunnel [luh toonel] 22
**tweezers** la pince [la pãs] 71
**typical** typique [teepeek]
**tyre** le pneu [luh pnuh] 25

**U**

**ugly** laid,-e [lay, led]
**uncle** l'oncle [lõkl] 13
**underground** le métro
[luh metro] 30, 31
**underpants** le slip [luh slip] 67
**underwear** les sous-vêtements
[lay soo vetmõ] 65
**unfortuately** malheureusement
[maluhruhzmõ]
**unhappy** malheureux (malheureuse)
[maluhruh (maluhruhz)]
**United States** les États-Unis
[layz‿aytaz‿oonee] 13, 80
**unknown** inconnu,-e [ãkonoo]
**urgent** urgent,-e [oorzhõ -t]

**V**

**valid** valable [valabl]
**value** la valeur [la valuhr]
**vegetables** les légumes
[lay laygoom] 46, 62
**very** très [tray]
**very much** beaucoup [bohkoo]
**vest** le tricot [luh treeko] 67
**video cassette** la cassette vidéo
[la kaset viday‿oh] 61, 67
**view** la vue [la voo] 50

**93**

**viewpoint** le point de vue
[luh pwã duh voo] 50
**village** le village [luh veeyazh] 22
**visa** le visa [luh veeza] 21
**visible** visible [veezeebl]
**visit** la visite [la veezeet] 49

# W

**waistcoat** le gilet [luh zheelay] 67
**wait** attendre [atõdr]
**waiter** le serveur [luh sairvuhr] 40
**waiting room** la salle d'attente
[la sal datõt] 72
**waitress** la serveuse [la sairvuhz]
**Wales** le Pays de Galles
[luh payee duh gal]
**walk** *(vb)* marcher [marshay] 56
**walk** la promenade
[la promuhnad] 49, 56
**wallet** le porte-monnaie
[luh portmonay] 79
**want** *(vb)* vouloir [voolwahr]
**warm** chaud,-e [shoh,-d]
**washing-up liquid** le produit à
vaisselle [luh prodwee a vaysel] 71
**watch** la montre [la mõtr] 66
**watchmaker** l'horloger [lorlozhay] 66
**water** l'eau [loh] 37, 39
**wave** la vague [la vag] 53, 55
**weather forecast** les prévisions
météorologiques [lay prayveesyõ
metayorolozheek] 19
**weather** le temps [luh tõ] 19
**Wednesday** mercredi [mairkruhdee] 19
**week** la semaine [la suhmen] 19

**weekdays** en semaine [õ suhmen] 19
**weight** le poids [luh pwa] 61
**welcome** bienvenu [byãvuhnoo] 14
**Welsh** gallois, e [galwa, -z]
**west** l'ouest [lwest] 22
**wet** mouillé,-e [mweeyay]
**white** blanc (blanche) [blõ (blõsh)] 20
**wide** large [larzh]
**wife** la femme [la fam] 13
**wind** le vent [luh võ] 19
**winter** l'hiver [leevair] 19
**wish** *(vb)* désirer [dayzeeray]
**witness** le témoin [luh taymwã] 27
**woman** la femme [la fam] 12
**wood** *(forest)* la forêt [la foray] 51, 56
**wood** le bois [luh bwa] 36
**wool** la laine [la len] 66
**word** le mot [luh moh]
**work** le travail [luh traviy] 14
**world** le monde [luh mõd]
**written, in writing** par écrit
[par‿aykree]
**wrong** faux (fausse) [foh (fohs)]

# Y

**year** l'an [lõ] 18, 19
**yes** oui [wee]
**young** jeune [zhuhn]
**youth hostel** l'auberge de jeunesse
[lohbairzh duh zhuhnes] 38

# Z

**zip fastener** la fermeture éclair
[la fairmtoor‿ayklair] 61

# French–English A–Z

# A

**à louer** for hire
**accès (aux quais)**
o the platforms
**adultes** adults
**aéroport** airport
**ambulance** ambulance

**A.P.E. (Assemblé Parlementaire
Européenne)** European Parliament
**arrêt** bus stop
**arrivée** arrival
**arrondissement (arr.)** district in Paris
**attention** warning
**autoroute** motorway

## B

**baignade interdite** no bathing
**banque** bank
**bibliothèque** library
**bicyclette** bicycle
**bienvenu** welcome
**billet** ticket
**blanchisserie** laundry
**boîte aux lettres** letter box
**boucherie** butcher's
**bouchon** traffic jam
**boulangerie** bakery
**bureau de poste** post office
**bureau de tabac** tobacconist

## C

**caisse** cash desk
**caisse d'épargne** savings bank
**carte** menu
**C.E. (Conseil de l'Europe)** Council of Europe
**centre (ville)** (town) centre
**chambre** room
**change** bureau de change
**chantier** building site
**chaud** warm, hot
**chaussée déformée** poor road surface
**chemin privé** private road
**coiffeur** hairdresser
**complet** (hotel) full; (theatre, cinema) sold out
**compris** included
**consigne** left luggage
**correspondance** connection

## D

**danger (de mort)** danger (of death)
**défense de ...** ... not permitted
**déjeuner** lunch
**département (dép.)** *département* (administrative division)
**destinateur** recipient
**déviation** diversion
**dîner** evening meal
**domicile** place of residence, home address
**douane** customs

## E

**eau non potable** not drinking water
**embouteillage** traffic jam
**entrée** entrance, admission price
**entrée gratuite** admission free
**entrée interdite** no entry
**entrée libre** please enter
**entrez** enter
**épicerie** grocery store
**état civil** marital status
**extincteur** extinguisher

## F

**fait main** hand-made
**fermé** closed
**feu** fire
**feu rouge** traffic lights
**fin d'interdiction de stationnement** end of parking restriction
**froid** cold
**fumeur** smoker

## G

**gare** station
**gazole** diesel
**gratuit** free

## H

**hommes** gents toilet
**hors service** not in use
**hôtel** hotel
**hôtel de ville** town hall (in cities)
**hypermarché** shopping centre

## I

**impasse** cul-de-sac
**informations** information
**interdit** forbidden

## J

**jour de repos** closed
**jour férié** holiday

## L

**lavabo** washroom
**lettres** letters
**libre** free
**libre-service** self-service
**location** rental
**location de bicyclettes** bicycle hire
**location de voitures** car hire

## M

**mairie** town hall
**marché** market
**menu** menu
**mer** sea
**messieurs** gents toilet

**métro** underground
**monnaie** (loose) change

**N**
**nettoyage (à sec)** dry cleaning
**non-fumeurs** non-smokers

**O**
**occupé** engaged
**offre spéciale** special offer
**office de tourisme** tourist information
**ouvert** open

**P**
**papeterie** stationery
**parking (gardé)** (supervised) car-park
**passage clouté** zebra crossing
**passage interdit** no entry
**passeport** passport
**péage** motorway toll
**petit déjeuner** breakfast
**piscine (couverte)** (indoor)
  swimming pool
**plage** beach
**plat du jour** dish of the day
**poissonnerie** fishmonger
**pont** bridge
**poste restante** poste restante
**pourboire** tip
**poussez** push
**priorité à droite** priority to the right
**privé** private
**propriété privé** private property
**prudence** caution

**Q**
**quai** platform

**R**
**ralentissez** slow down
**R.A.T.P. (Régie Autonome des
  Transports Parisiens)** Paris suburban
  railway network

**réduction** reduction
**renseignements** information
**respectez la priorité** give way
**retard** delay
**route nationale (R.N.)** national
  highway
**rue** road

**S**
**sens unique** one-way street
**serrez à droite** keep to the right
**signal d'alarme** emergency brake
**SNCF (Société Nationale des Chemins
  de Fer Français)** French railway
  service
**soldes** sale
**sortie** exit
**sortie de secours** emergency exit
**stationnement interdit** no parking
**syndicat d'initiative** tourist office

**T**
**tarif** tariff
**tarif réduit** reduced rate, reduced
  ticket
**T.G.V. (Train à Grande Vitesse)** high-
  speed train
**timbres** stamps
**tirez** pull
**TVA (Taxe à la Valeur Ajoutée)** VAT

**V**
**vacances** holiday
**virage dangereux** dangerous bend
**visite guidée** guided tour
**voie** track
**vol (intérieur)** (domestic) flight

**Z**
**zone de stationnement réglementé**
  short-stay parking
**zone piétonne** pedestrian zone

## Photo credits

All photos APA Publications with exception Werner Dieterich: 40, 53; Ralf Freyer: 17 (right); Rita Frunzetti: 65 (left); Thomas Gebhardt: 57; Herbert Hartmann: 37 (right.); Herbert Jennerich: 69; Annabel Elston/Apa Publications: cover.